10/93

Listening

to the

Candle

ALSO BY PETER DALE SCOTT

Poetry

Poems 1952
Rumors of No Law 1980
Prepositions of Jet Travel 1981
Heart's Field 1986
Coming to Jakarta 1988

Non-Fiction

The Politics of Escalation in Vietnam 1966
The War Conspiracy 1972
The Assassinations: Dallas and Beyond 1976
Crime and Cover-up 1977
The Iran-Contra Connection 1987
Cocaine Politics 1991

Translation

Zbigniew Herbert: Selected Poems (with Czeslaw Milosz) *1968*

Peter Dale Scott

Listening to the Candle

A Poem on Impulse

A NEW DIRECTIONS BOOK

Copyright © 1992 by Peter Dale Scott

All rights reserved. Except for brief passages quoted in a newspaper, magazine, radio, or television review, no part of this book may be reproduced in any form or by any means, electronic or mechanical, including photocopying and recording, or by any information storage and retrieval system, without permission in writing from the Publisher.

Manufactured in the United States of America
New Directions Books are printed on acid-free paper
First published as New Directions Paperback 747 in 1992
Pubished simultaneously in Canada by McClelland & Stewart, Toronto

Library of Congress Cataloging-in-Publication Data

Scott, Peter Dale,
   Listening to the candle: a poem on impulse / Peter Dale Scott.
      p.cm.
   Includes bibliographical references.
   ISBN 0-8112-1214-9
   I. Title.
PR9199.3.S364L5 1992
811'.54--dc20   92-4597
                                                              CIP

New Directions Books are published for James Laughlin
by New Directions Publishing Corporation,
80 Eighth Avenue, New York 10011

811.54
SCO

Dedicated to my mother
Marian Dale Scott

A NOTE ON READING THIS POEM

This poem has been written as a sequel to *Coming to Jakarta: A Poem About Terror*. Both poems are at times inscribed with quotations and glosses which many readers find distracting on a first perusal. In addition, readers at home in some parts of the poems will feel lost in others: an inevitable problem when poems attempt to generate and empower new audiences by breaking down traditional separations. I wish to encourage readers to seek a pleasurable rather than a disciplined experience, and to attend to and absorb only what rewards them. The sense of contextuality that the marginalia are intended to create is not one calling for immediate deciphering: what is initially obscure can remain obscure for as long as the reader wants. This is particularly true of *Candle*, a poem which meditates at the margins of language and consciousness, for "endarkenment" as well as for enlightenment. If the reader skips forward, postponing recalcitrant passages until he or she has browsed the entire poem, this will approximate to the non-linear way in which the poem has been written. This "poem on impulse," which like its predecessor took eight years to complete, now contains inscriptions and superscriptions which retard the poem's original spontaneities. The resulting paradoxes of time will be best experienced by a mimetic spontaneity of reading and, hopefully, re-reading. The Chinese marginalia in particular should not delay those who find them distracting: they will reward only those who have worked on reading the cited texts in the original. For that smaller audience, allusions to (e.g.) the Ox-Mountain parable of Mencius may help to enlarge a sense of unspoken presences within and beyond the poem.

I anticipate that some may be puzzled, or even disappointed, by this poem's relationship to its predecessor *Coming to Jakarta*. To them in particular I announce my hopes of finishing a third and final long poem. Thus the end of *Candle*, like that of *Jakarta*, should be seen not as a closure but as a transition, towards the completion of a trinal opus.

ACKNOWLEDGMENTS

As in the case of *Coming to Jakarta*, so *Listening to the Candle* has been helped by the sometimes necessary involvement of patient friends, too many to name. Prominent among them have been Kim Maltman, Roo Borson, James Schamus, Robert Pinsky, Frank Bidart, Robert Hass, Brenda Hillman, Amy Margolis, and Lisa Raphals. For the editing and production of the book, I must thank in particular Ellen Seligman, Sam Solecki, and Linda Williams of McClelland & Stewart, James Laughlin and Barbara Epler of New Directions. Over the years my chief indebtedness has been to Alan Williamson, and to the other poets of our Berkeley writing group: Chana Bloch, Sandra Gilbert, Diana O'Hehir, and Phyllis

Stowell. I also owe a big debt to my workshop students who have served as my teachers. The reckless process of impulsive poetics would have disgraced itself without their stern interventions. Finally, special thanks to all those, particularly P.L. Amin Sweeney, who helped in the great search for Javanese characters.

Listening

to the

Candle

I

I.i

For Adrienne Clarkson

No one ever had
        a fiftieth birthday quite like mine
    pointing a wooden

simulacrum of a Mannlicher Carcano
        from the sixth-floor window
    of the Texas School Book Depository

down into the green
        articulations of the oak trees
    on the way to the overpass

one attendant adjusting
        the small microphone on my lapel
    someone else measuring the light

the inscrutable TV hostess
        with whom I was to talk on camera
    mocking my academic style

the point of my squinting
        so closely down the barrel
    of the broomhandle or whatever it was

being precisely that from this window
        one could see almost nothing
    of the open limousine that was not there

and as there was more and more delay
        for additional light my eyes
    blurred even my ears

could make no sense of the voices
        I stared down this piece of wood
    that alone was in focus

and came to remind me
        not of why we were in Dallas
    but instead dimly of those years

this fear of losing control
        in that large world within us
    as I waited for a vastation

at last in that sultry smell
        of electricity
    before the cloudburst

at the top of a small Alp
        it seemed I had managed
    to fail out of my career

though in the end
        I lapsed into tenure
    unimaginable normalcy

and yet again for a moment
        this clumsy wood held in my
    hands becomes a weapon

futile against
the blurred vista of green

I.ii

For Daryl Hine

The snow has melted
   in the fields of Iowa
  white ditches

along the gridded roads
   and feathery furrows
  in reverse illusion

catching the light
   black ridges deep
  as archaeological excavations

where they catch the sun
   my mind too so reversed
  after the inconclusive

but very public
   debate with Colby
  about Indonesia and the CIA

that now it floats
   the dark fields of my inattention
  positively glisten

with rich fallowness
   why in maturity
  am I revisited

by those inner strains
   of alien certainty
  I failed to interpret

to my examiners at Oxford
   still whispering *Not this way!*
  and occasionally *This!*

leading in ways
        I cannot now imagine
    to the thundershaken dark peak

glistening not from rain
            but from the near electricity
    and the fear I could never reconcile

the voices murmuring within me
            with the small lightning without
    above the remote chapel

miles below at the bend
            in the deep canyon
    and four hours later followed

by thousands of trusting sheep
            whom I could only dispel
    by hurting them with stones

feeling the ironic power
        of a prophet fallen
    among the wrong chosen people

it was right that I knocked
            at the Italian border hut
    only to be placed under detention

one does not enter by this route
            a night of sleep under guard
    a sheepish return in their company

nothing in those weeks added up
            yet the very aimlessness
    preconditioning my mind

(after the debarkation
            in Montreal I do not remember)
    for blank lucrative hours

of sensory deprivation
        as a paid volunteer
    in the McGill experiment   *Heron 17*

for the US Air Force
        (two CIA reps at the meeting)   *Collins 48*
    my ears sore from their earphones'

amniotic hum my eyes
        under two bulging halves of pingpong balls
    arms covered to the tips with cardboard tubes   *Collins 50*

those familiar hallucinations
        I was first to report
    as for example the string

of cut-out paper men
        emerging from a manhole
    in the side of a snow-white hill   *Collins 51*

distinctly two-dimensional
        For two days they paid my mind
    to withdraw itself

from every impulse but its own   *Yeats '61 162*
        to look only on itself
    not seeing objects as objects

the humor of the darkness
        emboldening me to search
    deeper into silence

so I hitch-hiked north
        to the woods behind St. Sauveur
    it turned out my driver

was stopping with Jane's parents
        who as if worried invited me
    to spend the night

an invitation which if accepted
          might have saved me for normalcy
     and prevented that estrangement

from my efforts to return
          to that place of origin
     I had glimpsed in the experiment

and must go back to
          those limits of memory
     beyond learning to speak

that first lake
          in the Laurentians
     below the Northern Lights

of continuous darkness

                    I.iii

I had come back for recognition
          I was in no mood for aesthetics
     no one had told me a full moon

would emerge out of the shadows
          to highlight the jagged spruce
     like a Group of Seven canvas

above the wraiths of mist
          drifting slowly east
     across the glossy black water

no way now of course
          to remember that experience
     this very poem is like a house

to muffle the silent trees
        the mosquitoes that shone in the air
    like planes coming in to land

I had come here to be reminded
        that what you have to say
    is that you tell me nothing

and after two hours of mocking
        hoots and chuckles
    my own unkindred cries

in the moonlight thick
        as the flake white
    heaped up on my mother's palette

the drama was precisely
        to have made no closer approach
    I might as well lie down

why deal with the pictorial
        the croak of a nearby bullfrog
    is a wound in the shadows

and the small deathwatch beetle
        in the punk you sleep on
    keeps time close to your ear

counting the unknown number
        till the ant that explores your cheek
    is soon less unwelcome

than the ant you merely imagine
        or the pale zodiac
    of scorpions and long worms

that skate without pressure
        across eyeballs rigid
    from efforts to relax

and the fingers against your nose
    wink like fat glowing slugs
        until small eastern light

diminishes the shadows
    the night will end soon
        the fear of madness

become a foolish
    memento of the past
        and the nameless lake

become a mirror
    I don't mean that smoky surface
        still uttering mist

the heron lost in vapor
    but the whole landscape seen
        by a small naked boy

on a sunken log
    this visit no error but
        another erratic step

into a future
    so perfectly
        uninhabited

we call it home

II

Poetry is the past
that breaks out in our hearts
—Rilke

II.i

For Uncle Clunie and the Dales

Each morning
        for a few stolen minutes
    on *zafu* and *zabuton*   *cushion; mat*

beyond Maylie to the right
        I listen to the wet
    commuter traffic

the window occasionally trembling
        in front of my half-closed eyes
    as a truck changes gears

and six inches to my left
        the wall-silence
    a flatness not heard

till the sparrow's notes
        fall deeper inside my brain
    than I would once have dared

he was there then
        in the spindly sumac
    the granite too hard and old

for fossils or inscription
         my father is dying
     what would I have without these birds?

no language but breathing
         (the unheard gasp
     of water broken

by the small diving tern)
         the trees when I went back
     looked stunted in the lake

meadow and cabin gone
         except in my mother's oil
     a surprise above my uncle's

fireplace in the Pyrenees
         and I remember her easel
     in the garden by the primrose

now hanging in Clapham
         yellow ochre Prussian blue
     but why *crimson lake*

or the word *pitcher*
         when we found the pitcher plant
     still there twenty years later

slowly drowning its doomed flies
         in the swamp by the beaver dam
     on the trail to Mr. Pitcher's

I was to be drawn
         to this small carnivorous statue
     as if Mr. Pitcher himself

breakfasted on gnats
         while Elizabeth and I
     splashed mindlessly and naked

beside the grown-ups
          lounged on the makeshift wharf
     of unrotting cedars

a conspiracy of words
          I began to break into
     and make less ominous

the hot boring noon
          I said *fire fire*
     and they said *yes yes Peter fire*

but in the end my mother
          who talked and drank the least
     heard and saw me pointing

to the silvery pine root
          where russet needles turning
     to a bruise of white ash

had already browned a large
          hole in my father's
     too casually discarded shirt

these memories
          at the edge of language
     thin as worn canvas

acid soil a few weeks dense
          with pipsissewa wintergreen
     the rare lady's slipper

pitcher not *picture*
          dividing the world
     the cabin and meadow gone

into a picture
          no return to the soft
     water from that mossy

rainbarrel beneath the eaves
        my mother rinsing me
    that walk up under the balsams

to fetch drinking water
        clear as the sparrow's music
    above the lake

mind drifting with the clouds
        the bird I talked to
    until my grandfather

taught me why to hush
        and gladly I learned to dip
    the pail not my hand

in the leafy spring

II.ii

For Jori Smith and P.K. Page

I have flown north for a weekend
        again boots squeak on snow
    cold makes the stars larger

at St. Sauveur the tin
        steeple of the village church
    gleaming in moonlight

the ride from the ski train
        by horse and jingling sleigh
    under a bearskin

the colder the merrier
       faces lit from within
   my mother remembers the bells

of the sleighs on Sherbrooke
       the whirlwind of speed
   the voluptuousness of the cold   *Massie 366*

the smooth surface of the snow
       reflects the moon
   so that it is possible to read small print

flashes of the aurora
       in the north like spectres
   robes of the finest furs   *Collard 200-03*

even the excitement
       of the sudden snowstorm
   our poor pre-war Chevy

abandoned in the middle of Highway 8
       the road from Ottawa and Lachute
   a dozen or more strangers

huddling by the Quebec heater
       in the nearby farmhouse
   until the whirlwind blizzard died

the dark horses straining
       slowly through deep snow
   to the midnight railway station

those deliberate strong paces
       into that presence
   that cannot be the present

only enviable in recollection
       for travellers it was   *Massie 359*
   not unlike putting out to sea   *Collard 201*

immense caravans of sleighs
         100 to 150 together
     the manes and the beards of the men

have a particularly glittering effect   Massie 359
         or for a child that leafwork
     of frost on the double windows

in the blue sunlight
         the fun-loving empress
     had a glorious ice hill

at Tsarskoe Selo
         topped by a golden cupola   Massie 364-65
     My mother remembers

courtships of trammeled excitement
         the large can of cocoa
     in the smoky clubhouse

and the whirlwind blizzard's conversion
         from survival into art
     the street painted with new snow

the shovellers huddled
         under the haloed streetlight
     in my mother's painting

a miniature locomotive
         with a ruby headlight
     pulling the train

in the Great Siberian
         Railroad Egg   Massie 376
     when the frozen milk rose high

out of its glass bottle
         still wearing its cockeyed cap
     Patrick Anderson from England

with his stranger's eye
        fresh-froze it in my mind
     to outlast that pre-war era

on Oxenden Avenue
        when the horse that pulled the Elmhurst
     dairy wagon fell

on the ice and lay there
        they put a revolver in his ear
     my mother explained *his leg is broken*

and in 1918
        Fabergé asked only
     for ten minutes

to take his hat and leave
        he lived his last years in Cannes
     repeating over and over

This is not life

ALBUQUERQUE ACADEMY
LIBRARY

II.iii

For Charmian Reading

How important to escape
        from the sweltering asphalt
     to the meadow at Lachute

full of black-eyed susans
        the evening walk to Johnny Drennan's
     to stand on a pail

and turn the crank
        of the cream separator
     (I declined to milk the cows)

and home on Turkeycock Hill
            (avoiding the creek
        that ominous mudpuppy

with its lungs hanging out)
                to the low-flying whippoorwill
        that could be counted on

at bedtime
                and my dreams of falling
        changed by the discovery

or was it invention
                that I could fly
        Split cedar fences

had lain in the dune-grass
                for more than a century
        the rotted outline of the house

as we crossed the dunes
                I had made my kingdom
        every hillock named

my mother entering this empire
                of imagination
        called out *a coin! a coin!*

and it was—a French *sou*
                from the eighteenth century
        one glint of some human past

glamorously illegible
                and as for the present
        you can imagine my embarrassment

the day I walked up
                into the planted pine grove
        to find my mother

with her bohemian friend pegi
                both white-naked to the waist
        for which I should have been prepared

having been endlessly shepherded
                past the Modigliani
        in the Montreal Museum of Fine Arts

but Lachute after that
                was different I listened
        more to the talk of adults

Norman Bethune describing
                in his gravelly
        barrel-chested voice

why he would go to Spain
                the make-believe kingdoms
        mapped in the sand-dunes

my father's life
                of principled controversy
        now angrily challenged

letters for my mother
                with exotic stamps
        came from Barcelona

broad parchment folios
                with gothic script
        sepia notes and lines

saved by Beth
                for their illuminations
        red and blue angels

with faces prolonged
                around an *alleluia*
        the other leaves cut up

for improvised compresses
            in the monastery converted
        to an army field hospital

when we came back from Boston
            most of the pages had gone
        my mother not painting any more

natural appearances   *Shaul 31-32*
            evening primroses or squared
        log cabins in the Laurentians

but cubo-realist
            industrial elevators
        angular CEMENT

penetration into reality   *Shaul 31-32*
            my father playing Mozart
        and scanning the war headlines

Beth dying in China
            among the dying
        the new mysteries

that mostly could not be named

II.iv

For Natalie Fochs Isaacs

I wandered loonely as a cloud
            that floots on high o'er vales and hills
        but there was a war on

the draft-dodgers in the back
            of our male eighth-grade class
        interrupted the pure Scottish

lilt of Miss Hutchison's Wordsworth
          with rude whistles of air
     from inflated condoms

my first year in public school
          I was a blue serge Air Cadet
     marching with a wooden rifle

through the Westmount Junior High School gymnasium
          a small world enlarged
     by refugees from Berlin

Marianne who had me to *seder*
          under the dark Dutch art
     crammed in her parents' too small

living dining room
          (windows on scenes
     of that different world they spoke of

though never of their escape)
          and the dark Natalie
     black eyes and wide mouth

black curls all in disorder
          the age when a girl has ceased to be a child   *Tolstoy I, 39*
     for whom I read War and Peace

and imagined myself
          after one year away in Massachusetts
     as much a stranger as she was

or Bernie Schachtmann
          who at the insistence of the class
     was given the role of Shylock

when we read that *comicall history*
          The Merchant of Venice
     two tousand ducats in Frankford

much gratuitous comment
            when *Boinie*'s accent
       I vood my daughter were dead at my foot

and de jewels in her ear!   Merchant of Venice 3.1.75-79
            was deemed inadequately Jewish
       (all this at about the time

of Babi Yar)
            and cheers when the gracious duke
       gave Bernie no other choice

than be *content*
            to *become a Christian*   Merchant of Venice 4.1.380,385
       Shakespeare knew his crowds

who had just heard Dr. Lopez
            protest from the scaffold
       before *on doubtful evidence*

he *was publicly hanged*
            and quartered at Tyburn   Stirling 211
       that he had loved the Queene

as he loved Jesus Christ
            (which as Camden added
       from a man of the Jewish profession

was heard not without laughter)   Camden Annals, 1635, 431
            it was all very well
       that as our notes assured us

it was Shakespeare's art
            to write *If you prick us*
       do we not bleed or *The villainy*

you teach me I will execute   Merchant of Venice 3.1.56,62-63
            having sat with Natalie
       on the verandah

reviewing Latin
        rain in the trumpet creeper
    dripping heavily

with the language of desire
        I was too young to speak
    I could never again

quite forgive Shakespeare
        for the insularities
    of his complacent dukes

whose happy ending
        was *Get thee gone*   *Merchant of Venice* 4.1.395
    or to Caliban *Go to! Away!*   *Tempest* 5.1.299

bastard demi-devil
        and then the words enlarged
    by critics like Northrop Frye

into responsible wisdom *this thing*
        of darkness I acknowledge mine   *Tempest* 5.1.275-76
    and I could wonder in Quebec

if Shakespeare had spent one year in France
        could he have considered droll
    Katherine's *de fingre* and *de nick*   *Henry V* 3.4.50

or have made his happy ending
        out *of ten thousand French* men killed   *Henry V* 4.8.76
    now the English too had lost such numbers

as in the end such happiness invites
        One year away in Massachusetts
    and all rulers not just the Dauphin

but our own Mackenzie King
        seemed as alien as I did
    across an unseen border

their justice as exotic
      as Napoleon's armies
    arousing Natasha's lover Pierre

to some unformed act
      against the persecution
    of his country not yet strong

or as the Nazi jailers
      in my adolescent fantasies
    I protected Natalie against

awaiting the arrival
      of a world that had to be better
    And now still waiting

through yet more wars
      in the name of civilization
    after my much too long

delayed reading of the *Truyen Kieu*   *The Tale of Kieu*
      the national classic of Vietnam
    where the forces of law

are entirely destructive
      bailiffs going berserk
    for money's sake

cleaning out the household
      as is their custom   *Truyen Kieu* 578, 584, 597-98
    and the heroine Kieu

to cut down her father from the ceiling
      and save his neck from the cangue
    as Confucian piety demands

sold to a scholar-pimp
      and prostituting herself
    before our eyes   *Truyen Kieu* 685, 845

26

(something not even my adolescent
            daydreams were ready for
        though common now in Manila or Bangkok

child brothels around the U.S. bases   Seagrave 318-23
            Sex before 8
        or it's too late)   *San Francisco Chronicle* 1/30/91 A4

in which the happy ending
            is to accept karma
        talent and disaster go together

within us a root of good
            which outweighs our talents
        but must await rebirth

to redress the fluctuations of this life   *Truyen Kieu* 2788, 3247-52
            seas turning to mulberries and back
        every thirty years   *be-dau Truyen Kieu* 3, 715

a phrase still regularly quoted
            in meeting after Central Committee meeting
        O Shakespeare *nasz Shakespeare*   *our Shakespeare (Polish)*

I see at last
            however limited
        your quality of mercy

your refutation of Montaigne's
            case that cannibals have virtues
        (il y a plus de barbarie   *more barbarism*

à deschirer par torments et par gehennes   *to mangle by tortures and torments*
            un corps encores plein de sentiment   *a body full of lively sense*
        que de le rostir et manger   *than to roast and eat him*

aprez qu'il est trespassé   *after he is dead)* *Montaigne I, 183*
   you did not ease up on England's King *tr. Florio I, 223-24*
  model to England's *inward greatness*   *Henry V* 2pr.16

(What is't to me, when you yourself are cause
    if your pure maidens fall into the hand
   of hot and forcing violation

naked infants
    spitted upon pikes)   *Henry V* 3.3.19-21,38
  and I have cause to be grateful

your duke abjured his magic   *Tempest* 5.1.51
    set Caliban and his companions free *Tempest* 5.1.252
still more for the faith

of your Miranda
   quia impossibile
  O wonder

(because it is impossible)
how beauteous mankind is   *Tempest* 5.1.181-83

II.v

For Brenda Hillman and Robert Hass

It is all becoming
   coherent again
  as someone (Dogen?) says

arrival hinders arrival
    as we are we relax
  and things compose themselves

into the past and future
    a field of impulse
  the awkward time Ginky's

European governess
           found us in her bathroom
      or much worse when the patient

week-long investigation
           revealed that the culprit
      who completed the hole

in the partition wall
           between where the boys
      and girls changed for the class

called *rhythms* with Miss Bugnon
           leaping to Grainger
      was despite I fear denials

none other than myself
           (that was better forgotten!)
      these dead bees

make their own pattern
           on the cold zen-room floor
      honey the pleasure

arising from generation   Yeats '61 83
           blue hand on marmoreal nipple
      that breezy convertible

an inappropriate luxury
           for the driving snowstorm
      on Westmount Mountain

and our eroticism
           at odds with our world
      what impulse was it

in the gulf at Cacouna
           when I a small dot
      in my mother's Kodak

had to be rescued
          having wandered so far out
     in the lowest still tide

was it only
          the hush of the water
          the unseen opposite shore

or already a need to escape
          where a shoreline was drawn
     impulse effacing impulse

it is not the bell heard
          over the still water
          but the pulsing air

What ever happened to the Indians
          who would walk along the beach
     selling baskets and haircatchers

woven of sweet grass? my mother asked
          women
     knee-deep in the sea   *Lescarbot 47*

or the pleasure of digging
          a second well in the sand
     of the Lachute house basement

(as opposed to that wild moment
          in a voice not my own
     I told P to stop this small talk and undress)

two weeks in the near dark
          and at last the unmistakable
     dampness between the toes

or in bed the candle out
          the darkness
     behind thought

30

from which the present
                    is no more than
            the convex reflection

in a watery bead

                    II.vi

For Russell Brown and Donna Bennett

On that Westmount summit lookout
                    between the Precambrian
            and the cities of the plain

a feeling of being outside
                    on the margin of a presence
            rather than independent   Bennett 17

there seemed no choice
                    but either parochialism
            or grandiosity

Perspective! why I wonder
                    did a child being shown
            his last place at the edge

of the soot-streaked family tree
                    his grandmother in the wilderness
            recalling *the Maxwells of Munches*

seek no less than a descendence
                    from the Grand Dukes of Kiev
            the Roman consorts of the Merovingians?

while in school unable
                    to deal with peers
            who wrote of *the squirrel* or *the fox*

no he the only child
        of a left-handed mother
    had to embark upon a doomed

description of all the phyla
        the first of so many projects
    whose design was to be unfinishable

or years later on the cliff
        above the starlit
    grandly descending Manicouagan

all night guarding the flume
        for the Quebec North Shore Paper Company
    the vague sound of expectancy

from a vast river
        no one watched but myself
    beneath cold northern lights

J'suis le monarque   *I am monarch*
        de tout c'que j'vois   *of all I survey*
resounding from the cliffs

the choice of being
        diminished by what one sees
    to the point of anonymity

or enlarged by solitude
        to visions of madness
    flickering to the north

of the restricted regions
        where we deal in words
    going to England

(which is to say Univ   *University College, Oxford*
        to encounter the perspectives
    of Hamann the *Magus of the North*

Herder's defense of the primitive
　　　　　and belittlement of France
　　　　　from the ramparts of Königsberg and Riga

Hegel musing in the Alps)
　　　　　was traveling from the periphery
　　　　　to what was for me the center

it was the civilization
　　　　　that both gave the prompting
　　　　　and also the means

that enabled me
　　　　　to make that journey　　　　　　　　　*Naipaul 22-23*
　　　　　as Naipaul writes

contrasting the *Chachnama*'s
　　　　　unself-questioning celebration
　　　　　of the *plunder and destruction*

of the kingdom of Sind
　　　　　an article of the Arab faith
　　　　　that everything before the faith was wrong

to *our universal civilization*
　　　　　whose *philosophical diffidence*
　　　　　defines its strength　　　　　　　　　　*Naipaul 23-24*

and even Said (who might appear
　　　　　to be dissenting
　　　　　from my awareness

as a child in British colonies　　　　　　　*Said '79 25*
　　　　　at the margins of the west
　　　　　where race is no requisite

for *the feeling of being outside*)　　　　　*Bennett 17*
　　　　　for whom the *enlarged cosmopolitanism*
　　　　　of Western dominators

like Cromer and Baring
        could be traced to an *absolute*
    demarcation between East and West   *Said '79 37-40*

saw Auerbach's *synthesis*
        of Western culture
    risking *the possibility*

of appearing superficial
        and ridiculously ambitious   *Said '83 B 6*
    which possibly owed its existence

to being written in Turkey
        outside the Western academy   *Said '83 B 5*
    to the very fact of exile   *Said '83 B 8*

as an act of civilizational survival
        of the highest importance   *Said '83 B 6*
    matched by the unprecedented

gesture of doing it   *Said '79 259*
        the entire world
    a foreign land   *Said '79 259*

these wordless forests
        enveloping the city
    from which Northrop Frye

a megalomanic-depressive like myself
        wrote of the *peaceable kingdom*   *Frye '67 858*
    of reforging the broken links

between creation and knowledge   *Frye '57 354*
        though at first I spurned
    his partiality for the *eirenic*

to get clear of all such conflicts   *Frye '57 347*
        and dismissal of *revolutionary*
    action of whatever kind   *Frye '57 347*

as I did my father's
        at the time of HUAC   *Scott '91 16*
     yet his was the phantasy

of Orpheus and Virgil
        in a cabin beside a rapid
    conversing with Rousseau

Naipaul and Said
        our philological home
    is the earth

it can no longer be the nation
        the dream of discourse
    liberating by its constraints   *Auerbach '69 17: Said '83B 7*

to re-establish
        the original society
    of nature and reason

(now *overlaid by the*
        corruptions of civilization)
    with *a sufficiently courageous*

revolutionary act   *Frye '57 353; Scott '91 14*

II. vii

For Luther Allen, Chuck Kahn, and Susan Burgess

What I thought of at the time
        as *going insane*
    the conspiracy I now teach about

between luck and your own gut
        when your body has no choice
    but to live its rebelliousness

when uprooted to Paris
            fresh off the boat
      I lived in near isolation

from my old life of customs
            even my intention
      as a good socialist

to write about Jean Jaurès
            seemed more and more strange to me
      as I did myself

estranged by the bickerings
            in the student socialist cell
      (split that very year

by CIA dollars)
            I stopped going to classes
      and slept later and later

with more and more vivid dreams
            my waking life soon
      so tepid and insubstantial

it seemed a veil to *be torn aside*   Yeats '61 75
            before returning
      to the too-crowded station

the train that refused to leave
            (I must have the notebook somewhere)
      the small well-tied package

I found in a back lane
            of sleek butcher paper
      containing my grandfather's bones

which could be counted upon
            to fall disastrously apart
      in some public square

awakening me yet again
to the boring need
of filling myself with food

often more than I could do
to hear the voice beside me
when my one new friend

spent three hundred dollars on silk scarves
it was I who went out
to catch him in the lilacs

by answering his birdcall
under a full moon
I had stopped going to classes

when Luther and Chuck told me
in the *restaurant estudiantin*
they would cycle through the Dordogne

I at first declined
citing my non-existent work
the need to do something serious

and then Susan the stranger
at some rocky pass in her romance
showed guarded interest

the four of us escaped
by train all night from Paris
to the basilica at Conques

wedged in the narrow canyon
of apricot orchards
and its gold virgin

studded with cheap gems
the frightening
challenge of the Dark Ages

her stiff arms imploring
          like my own secret prayers
      like Susan's tears at Albi

when we failed to meet
          our two chaperones at the railway station
      her demand to be taken back

but after a sleepless night
          with our separate nightmares
      we continued south in a bus

that teetered ominously
          over a vast plateau with crags
      like angry dolmens the color

of the grazing sheep
          that seemed to have been here forever
      when at last we came down

to the bougainvilleas
          of the Mediterranean
      the *courses de taureaux*

in the Roman amphitheatre at Arles
          the view from our Gothic window
      in the hostel at les Baux

and to more and more trips
          the walk in the fog at Ruys
      the menhirs at Carnac

the oysters at Locmariaquer
          where after too much travel
      and at last nothing to say

we sat waiting for the ferry
          some part of me
      a caged panther

pacing my sub-awareness
   that six weeks later
  in a small Paris lobby

when you were late coming down
   for one more last
  futile meal together

would spill out
   onto the back of an envelope
  to my astonishment

suddenly the traces
   of an unexpected genealogy   *Stevens 50*
  my first publishable poem

the fatally familiar
   hotel room around me
  overshadowed

by the vivid unknown

II. viii

For Aunt Anna, Ann and Michael Keir

A small bedsitter
   off the Iffley Road
  no one that year in Oxford

paid less for their digs
   so cold I slept and ate breakfast
  in my monkish duffle

I was supposed to be studying
   the civil service
  but after Paul read the poem   *Paul Almond*

which had surprised me
        in a small Paris hotel
    he entered it in an *Isis* competition

judged by C. Day Lewis
        it took second prize
    I was invited

to a huge party
        thrown by the *Picture Post*
    for their feature on Oxford

the poet John B. Donne
        picked me from a crowd
    to wrap him in his cummerbund

everyone going to be photographed
        but I in my Eaton's suit
    shrank to the dark end of the hall

filling my dumb mouth
        with sherry in lieu of words
    and woke the next morning

lying in vomit
        Mrs. Jarvis telling me
    I would have to find new digs

but two weeks later in the *Post*
        next to J.B. in his attire
    there I was full length

one drink away from falling forward
        into Anne Younghusband's hairdo
    with *The Man*

Who Makes a Thing of Listening
        to underwrite two years
    of printed invitations

to champagne and strawberries
        from peers I had never met
    on the river lawns

beside the Isis
        as lesser men with their rented
        theatrical capes and gold-headed canes

muttered knowledgeably it was all
        a matter of whom you knew
    Paul whisking me away

on his motorbike to Stratford
        Io saro primo   *I will be first*
        e tu sarai secondo   *and you second Inf.* 4.14

(*Well that's what I remember*
        from your Dante class
    said a woman selling posters

in the Co-op lot)
        by his stronger will
    cast in the role of poet

Lewis and Spender our guests
        at the O.U. Poetry Society
    our receptions scintillating

with the flash of razors
        the unknown cutting the unknown
    while under the intense hands

of more serious successors
        our scruffy broadsheet
    became *The Fantasy Press*

my job to bicycle out
        with the latest copy
    to the lock at Eynsham

Oscar carefully
        disenvowelling one poet
    to publish another

while the long queues
        to speak in the Oxford Union
    discouraged me from emulating

Shirley Catlin's career
        I began to relax
    had a few nervous teas

with Elizabeth Jennings
        who clerked in the Public Library
    even Mrs. Jarvis allowed

me to stay on till June
        some inner reckoning
    had been postponed

my dons in Nuffield College
        down near the bus terminal
    studying administration

not into being *social*
        saw me as some Lucky Jim
    but in fact that whirl

was a slow disengagement
        from the successes
    I felt increasingly

had little to do with me
        that gap between the power
    to observe what was happening

and the self I read about
        in the *Isis* gossip columns
    replacing whatever

I had sailed with from Quebec
            the means of getting
        beyond what we think we want

the security of selfhood
to the poetry of luck

                    II.ix

        For Askold Melnyczuk

Walking out of the
            Bishop's Conference
        with the weapons makers from Livermore

at the Franciscan retreat
            below the field of poppies
        I saw *Songs from Taizé* on the piano

the monks at evensong
            in their white robes
        candles cupped in our hands

filing into the windowless
            twelfth-century village church
        I had come there by accident

but the following spring
            (while the painter Borduas
        fired for his *Refus Global*

with its *foi pour détruire*   *faith to destroy*
            *Refus de l'*INTENTION   *No to* INTENTION
        arme néfaste de la RAISON   *nefarious weapon of* REASON

                                            Borduas 111
took his refuge in Paris)
            I in flight from Oxford's
        efforts to civilize me

                    43

went back to La Pierre Qui Vire
        the wood of jonquils
    which Paul Crepeau and I picked

each day for the Virgin's altar
        rising in blackness
    stumbling to Matins

seemed right – a day in time
        opening to a timeless
    I seemed to hear more clearly

while Paul beside me
        prayed (as he confided
    years later to my father

Je priais   *I was praying*
        que votre fils   *that your son*
    ne soit pas converti)   *not be converted)*

but as sharply as whatever
        Provence landscape I saw next
    the bitter oranges

along the *country road*
        one must walk alone
    without even a dog as scout

to reinvent cadence   *Yeats '61 14*
        I recall the gentle laughter
    with the abbot's nod of permission

when the refectory lector
        chanted from the legendary
    of St. Catherine's miracles

in his well-pitched nasal tenor
        et de ses pieds   *and from her feet*
    il y sortait   *there issued perfume*

un parfum divin　　　　　*that was divine*
　　　O Borduas! I sought
　　　a church of tradition　　　　　　　　　　*Hyde 147*

you *une foi pour détruire*　　　*a faith for destroying*　　　*Borduas 111*
　　　each of us in revolt
　　　from our conflicting hegemonies

this search diminishing
　　　　the true dissonance of the everyday
　　　seeking what we could not

find at home in Quebec
　　　　at bottom the same thing
　　　a rupture with the present

une foi communiante　　　　　*a communal faith*
　　　　not *personnaliste* (like　　　　　　*Borduas 111*
　　　Marcel and Ngo dinh Diem)

but *community*
　　　　with what we experience
　　　within ourselves　　　　　　　　　　　*Yeats '61 69*

such matters of faith
　　　　now hopeless and undivisive
　　　they have brought out

Refus Global
　　　　in a university edition
　　　Place à la magie　　　　　*Make way for magic!*　　　*Borduas 51*

dégager le présent　　　*disengage the present*
des limbes du passé　　　*from the limbo of the past*　　　*Borduas 51*

45

II.x

For Sally Philipps Kavanagh and P. J. Kavanagh

The best truth
        is not enlightenment
    but kindness

anyone can learn
        in a day for a lifetime
    as I did on Wittenham Clumps

Sally shielding her eyes
        as she pointed across the Thames
    to the Vale of the White Horse

or touching my fingers
        to the raised welts of the poem
    carved in the bark

of an eighteenth–century beech
        a lover's complaint
    that will die when the tree does

I think she said
        the letters no longer legible
    and the archaeological journal

says *ruthless Danes*
        forgotten Cwichelm's grave
    such is the wreck which fate   Berks Arch. Journal IV (1898-99),
                                                                                                96, 123

She talked as if
        she were smiling at the world
    or singing Verdi

whom indeed she studied
        at her stepmother's in Milan
    her father waiting

to become the first Communist
　　　　　in the House of Lords
　　　she had received much

that would have spoiled others
　　　　　from those declining Apostles
　　　waiting in Chiltern manors

for their pre-war world to die
　　　　　and when I told her
　　　my don had warned me I would fail

they will say you're insane
　　　　　some crude unnegotiable certainty
　　　wrenching me from inside

she replied with a stillness
　　　　　so clear that when I have heard
　　　anything like it since

from others (coincidence
　　　　　they were all beautiful?)
　　　to this day my gut flutters

We walked down to lunch
　　　　　at her mother's house
　　　in Little Wittenham by the lock

filled with packing cases
　　　　　from the long-awaited marriage
　　　that was not going to happen

and again she took care
　　　　　as calmly of her mother
　　　as indeed of my own

colonial confusion
　　　　　at her friendship with so many
　　　I then thought famous

with speech clear
        and uncomplicated
    as the power of sunlight

to open flowers
        upright on their stems
    her face *pregnant with silences*

skeptical Derwent
        as we stood a decade later
    in the tall reeds of the Vistula

to hear the nightingales
        never one to fall for twaddle
    also acknowledging her grace

a way of laughing
        with the moon reflected
    in the rice fields

a residue
        of careful loving
    that must be given to others

I now believe anyone
        could have been confirmed
    with the wish to receive it

the ties of affection
        Twenty years later
    John Lehmann retailing yet again

his thin Bloomsbury gossip
        it was not worth trying
    to convey how his niece

made the world beautiful
        as the Cotswold churchyard
    above the triangular village green

Kavanagh
soave e piana Inf. 2.56

Inf. 2.127-31
Lehmann 98

Derwent May

恩情 *en[1] ch'ing[2]*

Lehmann 100

Lehmann 106-07

Hyde 70

with its quiet duck pond
   where by incredible chance
  (as I have just told Dekka   *Jessica Mitford*

at the party on Russian Hill
   for the dying Nora Astorga)   *Nicaraguan Ambassador*
  I and my Aunt Anna

whom I had told this tale at breakfast
   stumbled four hours later
  upon Sally's tombstone

the 24th year of her age
   the third of her marriage
  and I filled yet again

with the gratitude
   Sei immer tot   *Be forever dead Rilke '85 96*
  in mir   *in me Rilke '82 86*

of what has been received

     II.xi

   For Paul Almond

So much of my life
   has been a dialogue with you
  dear dead Sally

since that dangerous spring
   I kept preparing myself
  to fail the B. Phil.

and seemed to be sliding
   down the wet grassy slope
  of pleasure into madness

my poetry nothing but my prose
        imagining furious rejoinders
    to the reasonableness of my dons

and their political science textbooks
        proving *prophetic wisdom is harmful*
    impeding *the application*

of the piecemeal methods of science
        to the problems of social reform   *Popper 5*
    appeals to openness

I would not now cavil with
        rousing me to unexpected
    defenses of Burke's contract

not temporary and perishable   *Burke; Popper 111*
        argued incessantly in my mind
    at the top of the deserted

Kitzbuhel ski lift I would shout
        slogans from the *Phenomenology*
    to the winds below

my friendly tutor read my mock writtens
        and warned me of what I knew
    They'll say you're insane

but I went back to my volumes
        determined to betray neither
    my awareness of common sense

nor the increasing habits of words
        to press themselves through my mind
    for singing along strange rivers

to the discomfiture of songbirds
        in Wales or the Dordogne
    my footsteps an *obbligato*

nor the deeper instinct
        conducting me like a parent
    back to the vivid world

of those dreams in Paris
        external voices like my own
    could only warn me against

but now my neediness
        was sensed by kindly women
    the much photographed Caroline

the down-to-earth Shirley
        Renata the potter
    who made a dish for me

and kissed me behind the kiln
        even Peg who brought me
    my flounder and chips at the Lantern

hinting how good
        a man's sex felt inside her
    I liked the sound of that

but went on reading my Hegel
        on the plastic tablecloth
    (it was years later in Montreal

reminiscing with Paul and Tom
        about the Oxford good life
    I finally caught her drift)

when M wanted to join
        my tracking of D.H. Lawrence
    over the frontier Alps

I arranged for her to hitchhike
        with my cousin Rosemary
    who had just broken her engagement

so I could be alone
            with my defiant *clichés*
        le coeur a ses raisons   *the heart has its reasons*

que la raison ne connaît point   *which reason knows nothing about*
            the Wicksteed Dante
        stuffed in my rucksack

to be read while waiting for rides
            there where the snow freezes
        blown and packed by the winds

dissolved, drips into itself   *Purg.* 30.88
            but my last night in Oxford
        all principles in disarray

caught between the risks
            of belonging to the world
        and the risks of being ourselves

I a near virgin
            allowed my body to be used
        by M's in need

in a mutual anticlimax
            (*Is that all there is to it?* she asked)
        which was also relief

I kissed her and left
            for the illuminated
        railway yards beyond

the old marmalade factory
            knowing that I had failed
        not only Oxford

but more importantly to go mad
            stubbornness protecting
        some inner certainty whose value

is still in question
            appeased by the very randomness
        of a life defying control

I watched from the train windows
            moonlight fading to dawn
        the cranes of Southampton

and still sleepless a few hours later
            on the broad steamer hatch
        I thought back with full heart

to the two Italian beauties in Sterzing
            who had mocked my neediness
        Why would you travel so far

away from home alone?
            and before that on the Alp
        looking down into the Sudtirol

between the sheet lightning above
            which raised in me
        audible fear

and underfoot
            the dwarf
        purple cyclamens

there are times when meaning
            is so profound
        one is indifferent to happiness or death

as in that small hailstorm
            a space where they might have seen nothing
        but I had touched

the limits of my mind

II.xii

The lake beyond language
                    the place Maylie and I
                    (having lost my old topo maps

and my mother too frail
                    to come into the forest with us
                    waiting by the car)

failed three years in a row
                    to come back to
                    the road through the spruce and maples

soon only leaves
                    between two stone fences
                    then a deer trail in club moss

that could no way lead me back
                    to that paralysis of failure
                    those drifting presences

the black mists
                    the white listing firs
                    the silent water

where there had never been
                    so much as the echo
                    of one lost Touraine folk song

let alone a Scots ballad   *Steiner 316*
                    that perhaps
                    most important night of my life

I refused the concerned
                    invitation of the Reeds
                    to join their artists' party

and walked back into my past
        that absence we call *nature*
      that absence from which we have effaced

the Indian city dancing
          lesquelz nous apportoient   *they brought us*
      pain fait de gros mil   *bread of large grains*

lequel ilz jettoient   *which they threw*
        dedans nozdites barques   *into our boats*
     en sorte qu'il sembloit   *till it seemed like*

qu'il tombat de l'air   *a shower from heaven*   *Lescarbot 440*
        and that lake whose silence
      I still considered

my first home
         (les femmes nous vindrent   *the women came*
      baiser le visage   *and kissed our faces*

pleurans de joye de nous voir   *weeping for joy to see us)*   *Lescarbot 443*
        the traceless surface
      of still older violations

(ilz le tuent   *they kill him*
         l'incisent par les fesses   *slash great gashes in his hips*
      l'avallent au fond de l'eau   *sink him to the bottom of the river*

puis le retirent à-mont   *then draw up the body*
        et trouvent dedans les taillades   *and find in the gashes*
      lesdits Cornibots desquelz   *the said river-pearls whereof*

ilz font de patenôtres   *they make beads*
        comme nous d'or   *as we do gold*
      la plus précieuse chose   *the most precious thing)*
                          Lescarbot 442
that long significant night
        of nothing at all happening
      grateful at first for escape

from ghosts who failed to materialize
              and later to have got outside
        the constrictions of what then appeared

to be normal life
              and later still for the proximity
        to unspeakable shadows

(the Ox-Mountain parable of Mencius   *Mencius 6A:8.1*
              without the night spirit   氣 *ch'i⁴ breath*
        that breathes out of the darkness

human nature cannot be itself)   *Merton 137*
              the lake a wall of silence
        the shadflies rising silently

from the motionless creek
              When the Inuit mother
        is in labor

an old woman says
              as many names as she can think of
        the child comes out of the womb

when its name is called   *E. Carpenter 39*

III

She opens her mouth with wisdom, and the teaching of kindness is
on her tongue.

—Proverbs 31.26

III.i

At the intense party
                of transient laughter
        I am unable to speak

and when someone presses me
                I tell them my first wife
        Maylie has died—wild

sobs then such as I
                can no longer summon as I did
        enough to wake me up

and feel her asleep beside me
                and unreachable
        It was yesterday's picnic

for Maria's graduation
                Ruth the eighty-four-year-old
        German Jewish emigrée

whose husband had been best friends
                with Walter Rathenau
        murdered close to their home

and whose daughter had not told them
                of the Rector's edict
        that students should maintain

a distance of three steps
           between themselves and the Jews
       on the school staircase

distressed she could not remember
           the name of her first boyfriend
       the world-famous novelist

I said *My father is your age*
           I would be so glad
       if his memory were like yours

differences collapsing
           his home a hospital bed
       his wry smile

when I said to him *Good!*
           for finishing his Jello
       our two faces together

with an absurd spoon
           and my wondering for a moment
       if I could go on speaking

just like once or twice
           in the months after Oxford
       no matter how much we conceal it

we give our best love
           to those who are going to die
       the scars we receive from life

now more than we wish
           protecting us against death
       as holes begin to spread

through life's tapestry
           the blur we see around us
       of dianthus and rhododendrons

this champagne with still more strangers
        whose very accessibility
    is the mark of estrangement

or to read Adrienne Rich
        About the time my third child was born
    what frightened me most

was the sense of drift
        I seemed to be losing touch
    with whoever I had been
                                       Rich 354

A friend's bedridden wife
        another grotesquely fat –
    these are not my problems –

Maylie stirs with her own dream
        disturbing if like mine
    it gives back what we black out

the peace between us
        from separateness
    expensively acknowledged

no longer the tennis partners
        of those frighteningly
    innocent photographs

with no hint of the hidden rules
        to the game being played
    Maylie up in the apricots

we picked for a week
        with migrant laborers
    in the valley of the Okanagan

Everyone
        should have to do this
    feeling the slow heat

of summer ripening into autumn
        as if this branch
    were some deep memory

(first the shadow
        then the bird itself
    without a wing beat)   *Merton 246*

heavy with fruit so soft and sweet
        as to be no good for commerce
    and only eaten now

as if the ladder against the branch
        stood now from trust by itself
    as if the whiteness

of the snow on those mountain peaks
        were the forgiveness
    for the different ways

in mutual silence
        (not age but release
    from that kind of future)   *Rich 355*

we have both gone on changing
        each to more inward
    solitary landscapes

her dawn at Tassajara
my dusk on Capitol Hill

III.ii

For Selma Huxley

That return to a winter of survival
        at a small school
    in the fields and mountains

teaching children in what seemed
        a sort of penance
   but also the comfort of having

no large schemes in mind
       as I walked through the foothills
   in my surplus army khakis

singing *non e cosa in terra*   *there is nothing on earth*
       che ti somigli   *which resembles you Leopardi*
   or quoting Gregory *what*   *quid*

does this world teach us   *aliud quam*
       but that we should not love it?   *ne diligatur clamat?*
   the woods purpling in the distance   *Dialogues 3.38*

I must from unthinking
       have had contempt for life
   the drunken hunters'

bullet chattering through the leaves above me
       or in the untracked snow
   in momentary terror as the stag

sprang out from under the spruce
       flooding my eyes with fresh powder
   I had felt a guilty silence

Perdidi musam tacendo   *I have lost my muse by not speaking*
       (the city behind me   *Pervigilium*
   coke ovens reddening the clouds)

but the shock of the duck's
       blood in the frozen reeds
   every step in those deep

and uneventful woods
       had the sense of being predestined
   that whole year I lived with

enormous distance between desires
        and their objects
      the slow alterations of sunrise

the swifter alterations of the moon
        as I studied Rilke's
      lieben heisst allein sein   *to love means to be alone*   *Rilke '82 84*

the anglophile schoolmaster
        who had never been east of Quebec
      forcing us to play cricket

and attend evensong
        (each night ten verses – exactly – of a psalm
      Non nobis Domine   *Not to us O Lord*

sed Nomini Tuo   *but to your name*
      da gloriam   *give glory*   *Psalm 115:1*
      and then John Chrysostom

grant those wishes of your faithful
        as may be expedient for them)
      who failed my best student in my absence

for not knowing the proper
        salutation to address a bishop
      and then while waiting

like the trees outside
        for the small brightly-tinted
      warblers from Costa Rica

again to dart from the overhanging
        branch to the sheltered pool
      bloodroots and trilliums

to whiten the black earth
        the deprivation
      I had anticipated with fear

turned to a simplicity
          some enjoyment of a direction
      not wholly to be diverted

as for example when J
          whose hands by trembling
      had once made mine tremble

drove up to visit
          could we swim naked
      in the headmaster's lake

now that she was married?
          and at the school-year's end
      on my return to Montreal

new friends in the province singing
          the new songs
      of miners and asbestos strikers

and as in a romance
          as if a reward for timing
      in silence and speaking out

you came from nowhere
          and made it possible
      to live in the city

the pace of the forest
still inside

III.iii

For Louis Dudek and Aileen Collins

My father had come back
          to civilize Montreal
      with Medici prints

Djwa 77

the sepia del Sarto
        the *Blue Boy* in blue
    my mother's reservations

followed by WORKERS WORKING
        and then in the post-war
    reconstruction which this time

had to be really different
        a preoccupation with generative
    forms like CELL AND CRYSTAL

and also openness
        or what Sir Herbert Read
    called *non-directed thinking*   *Read 192*

while Louis Dudek
        returning from the turbulent
    encounters at St. Elizabeths   *H. Carpenter 800-03*

to our more restricted
        realm of the possible
    at the wilderness' edge

(where marginality itself
        with so few of us
    to cope with cultural crisis

created a phantasy of power
        and responsibility
    unimaginable in New York)

tried to civilize the
        still winter-dark city
    with the first visits

of Auden Dylan Thomas
        and the evenings in our homes
    when Cid Corman would hitchhike up

with the latest scraps
        from the Black Mountain school
    committees of correspondence

still united for cultural
        innovation but tamed
    Creeley's *the grey*

hat bought earlier sickens   *Creeley '62 39*
        to a more circumspect posture
    John Sutherland's *Northern Review*

after Gouzenko's revelations   *Stevenson 311*
        migrating from the CP
    to Catholicism and tuberculosis   *Woodcock 54*

the new glass skyscrapers
        of the new cosmopolitan city
    casting their neutral shadow

over Mount Royal with its cross
        while millions of schoolchildren
    were taught *Lord of the Flies*

(the legacy of Hobbes
        though what Kropotkin
    had remembered of Darwin

was the blind pelican
        whose comrades kept him
    supplied with fish)   *Hyde 92*

the *Montreal Renaissance!*
        Alarmed by the neglect of classics
    we urge that the student ask

what part of the author's discoveries
        is likely to be of use
    in maintaining the life of the mind   *CIV/n 114*

In Montreal Dudek remembers
      we were laughed down
    for "trying to bring about

civilization"   *Dudek 103*
      but it must have rubbed off on me
    as I struggled with Eliot

the reunification of the world
      and of the individual
    may be one and the same

in this *contrée énorme*   *enormous country*
      où tout se tait   *where all is silent*   *Breton 60*
    languages religions

once the vehicles
      of a nation's coherence
    now forcing it apart

in an emergence to power
      and simultaneous dissolution
    but no one from the States

can imagine what this illusion
      of totality was like
    to have written not just for the sake

of self-expression or for that
      matter *the extinction of personality*   *Eliot '32 17*
    but from the needs of a mute

community to be distinguished
      by a spirit of engagement
    with an alien tradition

that ambivalence towards the past
      which once led Virgil to refine
    the arts of *others* (meaning the Greeks)   *Aen. 6.847*

or Spenser to recreate
        and then destroy with vengeance
    his Italianate *Bower of Blisse*   *Faerie Queene* 2.12

or in the '50s to Reaney's
        gracefully up and downing
    merry-go-round of Mopsus   *Reaney 42*

from that sense of
        opportunity and crisis
    that comes from deprivation   *P.D. Scott '91 22*

shared by a handful
of enemies and friends

III.iv

For K

Electric with desire
        from the possibilities
    of my new adult flesh but also

in fear of drowning
        I fled my birthplace
    into a foreign marriage

renouncing the *alte Feindschaft*   *the ancient enmity*
        zwischen dem Leben   *between life*
    und der grossen Arbeit   *and the great work*   *Rilke '82 84*

Ist es nicht Zeit dass wir liebend
        uns vom Geliebten befrein
    is it not time that we loving

free ourselves from the loved one —
      (so true but so precocious
  before those twenty

or so years needed
      for one's family to ripen)
  I am reminded of

when kissing J good-bye
      and all these sudden memories
  like the matted roots

one meets each spring
      redigging the vegetable garden
  and then forgets again

like the dream forgotten
      the instant we wake
  whose only trace

is that our walk into daylight
      is *a walk on depths*
  from which understanding

less painful than love
      proclaims the presence
  of this other world

not just escape from history
      but good history's center
  what we truly care for

out of the dim past
      J's flashing whiteness
  squirming like a caught fish

in the hot Tennessee lake
      suddenly darkened by a rainstorm
  the more exquisite pornography

and more lily whiteness
              of that other much earlier J
        struggling to give herself

as far as humanly possible
              from the cramped bucket seat
        of her flimsily hooded MG

in the snowblack Canadian night
              What heat in her chilled breast
        what flame in that half-numb hand

and at that poets' party
              I haunted by fantasy
        Dylan's hand in young corsages

prepared to rehearse the role
              of my friend who'd memorized Rilke
        lieben heisst allein sein   *to love means to be alone   Rilke '82 84*

to assist in his seductions
              the expansiveness
        of imperial selfhood

among those eager to worship
              but when my best friend's wife
        the sexiest woman in Montreal

confronted me in the basement doorway
              with my dream *you know I love you*
        I armed with only

the courage of my inhibitions
              knew it was time to flee
        not just my mother country

like Eve glad to have
              a chiding angel but
        (as when the sun rises

later and further south
            it is actually closer
            the cold is from the earth

in its winter tilt away)
            also the apparition
            of that too familiar career

the national poet
            of becoming a local personality
            drugged by too much flesh

to be in touch with
            the workings
            of the ocean of the world

one must be
            tinged with nothingness
            along with the past

as in a snowstorm
            no two snowflakes the same
            each recording *the history*

of all the changing
            weather conditions it has experienced   New York Times 1/6/87;
            so *each political event*   Cumings 3

is both structured and random   Cumings 4
            this need to crystallize
            a unique otherness

like *the choices made*
            by the branching tips   New York Times 1/6/87; Cumings 3
            without thinking of it

without suspecting the world
            and the marriage
            about to be commenced

apart we rotted in luxury
        adored & spoiled by lovers
    together the simple couple   *Plath '83 154*

I lleft my country
        in response to *temperature*
    humidity

or impurities in the air   *Cumings 3*

                III.v

        For Leonard Cohen

What we are is not just our past
        but what we choose to remember
    those more sensitive

recalled the queer sultry
        electrocution of the Rosenbergs   *Plath '72 1; '82 80*
    (the secret intercepts

from William Stephenson's Camp X
        in a safely Tory Province
    far too sensitive

to be exposed at a trial)   *Stevenson 19*
        or the launching of *Encounter*:
    to believe them *falsely condemned*

one would have to believe the judges
        monsters insensate beasts   *Fiedler 20-21*
    but the following spring

as the Korean War subsided
        the students of Eliot House
    gathered each morning round the TV

cheering Welch against McCarthy
it was as if each of us
personally and with strangers

was waking from a nightmare
and a shared craving for decency
allowed us again to speak

TV presenting the *field*
without *the lyrical*
interference of the ego   *Olson 156*

the old linearities of judgment
my mother having finished
ATOM BONE AND EMBRYO

with more *process* and impasto   *Olson 148*
was painting FIELD
and now Drew Pearson

who had leaked the Gouzenko story   *Stevenson 145*
spoon-fed to him by Stephenson   *Pilat 202*
turned and helped *put Joe McCarthy*

out of commission   *Pearson 541*
whatever the details
the great shoot-out seemed over

the Cold War turned around
I began that spring to conceive
I could finish my timely thesis

on *la diminution*   *the diminution*
des traces   *of the traces*
du péché originel   *of original sin*   *Eliot '32 392*

and took time off for lunches
with the Harvard poets
of the *School of Charm*   *Breslin 52*

74

always airy and sunny
> as the Mediterranean
> piazzas of their poems

it was an age for Stevens
> *the truth that we experience*
> *when we are in agreement with reality*   *Stevens 59*

turning to Frost's *golden*
> *age of poetry and power*   *Eberhart 207, 212*
> an age of rhyme

the *virtue of meaninglessness*   *Wilbur '76 222*
> an age when nobody
> least of all Adrienne Rich

seemed to confront anyone else
> as they gossiped about I Tatti
> *part of happiness*

to converse as it were
> *with the whole of tradition*   *Wilbur '66 484*
> making my trips back north

to the last-ditch manifestoes
> of *CIV/n* against the world
> or east to the backbiting

gossips of Rathbone Place
> dissecting Dylan Thomas
> seem like a time-warp

the poet increasingly
> *disposed* in this decade
> *to think of himself as citizen*   *Wilbur '76 115*

(the governments *needed legitimacy*
> *which was provided*
> *by the so-called "creative" writers*)   *Herbert '87 559*

Louis whose first tour *Louis Simpson*
        of Europe was no holiday but a war
    recalled *there were not men*

living in those days
        but masks
    aspects of the New Criticism *Simpson 165*

but what do you expect
        when you have had two wars
    twice the end of an era

and then an interlude to marry
        and have perhaps three children
    Lenny Cohen saying

on the long drive down to Boston
        what do you believe in then?
    and thinking myself

original in digging up
        what was in fact
    the slogan of the decade

I answered *survival*
        even Allen Ginsberg
    defying the taboo

against grandiosity *Breslin 106*
        by writing *Howl*
    real holy laughter in the river!

was in a sense
        following Stevens
    the brilliance of earth

is the brilliance of every paradise *Stevens 77*
        to proclaim the 道 Tao
    against dialectic

America
> *it is you and I*
> *who are perfect*

not the next world

III. vi

For Gene Skolnikoff

From our last costly trip
> to Acoma and the Grand Canyon
> nothing but the place mats

placed in silence
> by you each morning on the table
> while I by the same code

set out the milk carton
> with the face of the missing child
> and with hardly a word

(how could I foresee
> that in the end what you would thank me for
> was my leaving you alone)

we eat our cereal
> above these cheap reproductions
> of the Colorado

the latest keepsakes
> like the self-important album
> in which long ago

we naively pasted
> photo after photo in rows
> with exact dates and places

now totally forgotten
        the dense carpet of gentians
     under our aching feet

still that small raft in my mind
        which ferried us out of childhood
     against a blurred horizon

and the later photos loose
        in manila envelopes
     ourselves with our three grown children

in some more recent mountain pass
        our smiles for some stranger
     concealing separateness

that only emerged
        when once again
     there were only two of us

but is it less natural than
        dedication in youth
     to be separate in old age?

joy snapshots
        like escapes into mindfulness
     are too swift for epics

even Dante found it easier
        to write about
     the ineffable shape of God

than about his marriage
        and Rilke wrote
     that love is *letting go*   *Rilke '82 84*

meaning the opposite
        of what love meant for me
     letting go of the patriarchal

summons to greatness
        that love of perfection
   which had kept me apart

cultivating my cherished
        contemptus mundi
   Why should I trust this world?

reading Baudelaire
        for his *certitude*
   de faire le mal
                                    Eliot '32 390

St. Paul's reminder
        There is none righteous
   no not one
                                      Romans 3:10

and praying fiercely
        until the fatal view
   of the Franciscan oblate

kneeling in front of me
        with pointed Gucci shoes
   under his vestments

For our third date
        we arranged to have dinner
   and to our relief instead

went skating on Spy Pond
        with Gene who had a car
   so intent on getting married

who with considerateness
        I had not yet learned
   took the time (as I recalled it)

to improve your balance
        (though in your memory it was
   to console you after my inept

defensive near-rebuffs
         to the risk you offered
      of happiness at hand)

while I rushed towards the dark
         far side of the pond
      trying vainly to keep stride

with the buried thunder
         of the ice dropping beneath me
      old Quebec sound

under northern lights
         spruce tree cracked by frost
      the echoes of solitude

that will always be there
         if one needs to hear them
      and then back to the half-light

from the parking lot
         Gene our Galeotto
      still gliding you shakily forward

a life-size emblem of life
         into those spaces
      for ourselves and our children

we could never have planned
         the small story of our marriage
      still even as we move

out beyond it
         a coming to focus
      for twenty or thirty years

on ordinary life

III. vii

For Allan and Sondra Gotlieb

The Canadian middleness
> *where war was*
> *there let ego be*

inspired us young bureaucrats
> gladly to sacrifice
> our separate intelligences

for an *esprit de corps*
> to derive what pleasure one could
> from the imposition of reasonableness

in your case make legislative
> arrangements for the bottom of the sea
> that would have saved many endangered

species if implemented
> in my case put inventory
> labels on the bottom

of the ambassador's furniture
> once or twice ride through crowds
> with the Canadian flag fluttering

but how elegant at night
> those talks in the Diplomats' Lounge
> about Rumi and al-Hallaj

at ease with all the dharmas
> unaware that money
> from Saudi oil

had marginalized Sufism
> for its *values essentially*
> *outlawed by the main*

system of Islam   *Said '79 272*
          (nothing but glass
     between us and the East River

tenements of Brooklyn
          from which five years later
     a Cuban exile nationalist

with the right CIA drug connections
          would fire a bazooka)   *Hinckle 321*
     or about art with Tambi

the Sinhalese publisher
          of Olson's *Projective Verse*
     (his hair no longer wild

as it had been in London
          where he broke up P's marriage
     by getting M pregnant)

who had turned up there
          (We are increasingly becoming
     a world of migrants

made up of bits and fragments)   *New York Times 2/23/89 B2*
          with the wife of Professor Pearson
     who recruited for OSS   *Office of Strategic Services*

or the Peekskill weekends
          where hostesses arranged
     for us to shoot their frightened duck

wheeling in consternation
          in the red sunlight
     above the small pond

that had been their home
          as the well-fattened M.P.   *Member of Parliament*
     demonstrated at excruciating length

his impotence with a gun
           I was being saved
      from myself by adjusting

to a divided civilization
                all we can do is take
           these different shapes

of Jew and Christian and Muslim   Rumi '86 83, 21 (1325, 321)
           the important thing
      as I learned from my superiors

to suffer fools gladly
           to judge a little less
      surtout pas trop de zèle!   *above all don't be too earnest!*

as when the M.P. turned out
           to be an opera lover
      and took me to *Eugen Onegin*

art lessens our definitions
           when I read the NATO document
      so secret it would have been illegal

for me to divulge even
           its classification
      I said to my boss

but how do we know there are
           one hundred seventy-five
      Soviet divisions?

and Ray just back
           from his trip with Pearson to Sikkim
      looked quizzically at me

over his tented fingers
           (across my mind at that moment
      the trace of a bird in flight

A Zen line: Is it by your wisdom
            that the hawk soars?)
    his silence making clear   *Merton 285; Job 39:26*

that if I was serious
            about wanting to join
    this bureaucratic tribe

I like everyone else
            must honor its taboos
    Now that was a discovery

in the bureaus of *reasonableness*
            while artists were being paid
    to support the public illusion

that *Nothing was sacred*
            with *deliberately transgressive*
    work of nose-thumbing daring   *New York Times 2/23/89 A6*

as the Muslim responded
            to Salmon Rushdie
    one selects not to mislead

but to make more meaningful
            this subject
    is deadly serious

and to make it a subject
            of insensitive fantasy
    is equally serious   *New York Times 2/23/89 A15*

on midsummer eve
            shortly before I left
    the Foreign Service

thousands of us stood
            on the Most Poniatowski   *Poniatowski Bridge*
    across the Vistula

84

and looked upstream
         to the descending fleets
     of candles little lamps

even rafts afire
         having to do with good luck
     an observance perhaps

from before St. John
         so trivial even the party
     officials could be present

we have never really left
anywhere we have been   *New York Times 2/23/89 B2*

III. viii

For Cassie

Rush home for dinner
         between a poetry reading
     and a public lecture on peace

and since Maylie
         is once again absent
     on one of her five-day *sesshins*   *sittings*

I expect the kitchen to be deserted
         but no! Cassie fresh
     from her twenty-fifth birthday party

is there and sees right off
         a moment to pamper
     fixes some food while I relax

even though it may be
         we shall always be awkward
     there being more forethought

to the strangest arranged marriage
            than when father and daughter
    first look on each other

nothing those first years
            of whirlwind diplomat parties
    or canoe trips in the Laurentians

prepared us newlyweds for
            (the French pregnancy movie
    had counseled an energetic life)

a morning hike up a waterfall
            in the middle of the night
    a silent tight-lipped drive

and then suddenly Cassie
            five weeks premature
    no more than a 4.5 pound

baby koala
            in the palm of the nurse's hand
    How many shocks in life

can there be like that one?
            never before had I felt
    responsibility for such pain

as your misery and rage
            emerging from the ether
    of surgery at six weeks

the months of colic
            you could only be pacified
    by long drives on country washboard

or the nurserybook moment
            behind the hill
    just this side of the Iron Curtain

geese crossing the cobblestones
              a screech of brakes
        and you still smaller than your bear

ended up at the bottom
                of a pile of cribclothes
        on the Peugeot back-seat floor

pains I would like to blame
                for your subsequent anger
        and not those later years

of crisis meetings books
              that always brought me home
        at dinner time too late

to pass through the small door
              of your wonderland
        to be a good father

I tried hard to live
              a life without scandal
        in the end that too failed

along with that future
              I wasted your childhood on
        but tonight you make no issue of it

tonight some instinct remembers
              the long vigil in Warsaw
        the Vistula frozen and so

no water heat electricity
              by candlelight we clutched you
        through your hot terrifying fever

to the dull booms
              as they dynamited the ice
        or when our Peugeot skidded

in the Silesian snowstorm
           stopped only by the kilometer stone
      its back wheels hanging in space

Maylie's sure hand scooping
           you without hesitation
      instantly out of the back seat

the same involuntary way
           Maylie's flesh became your milk
      her hair straightened

and across her sweet breathing *hara*   *belly*
           there appeared stretchmarks
      Once you had been born

we could no longer as before
           want only for ourselves
      just as now we must unlearn

that intense involvement
           which served to make us more sane
      than our earlier freedom

nothing like that unique
           response to my first glimpse
      of your half-alien redness

of being despite illusions
           of identity and choice
      no more than the outer flesh

of some buried seed
           whose great singlemindedness
      had for a brief generation

used us and our desire
           as it might yours
      and if this has not

88

informed me with the skill
        to put easily into words
    I love you

nevertheless I feel the gift
        of this added force
    the more gratifying

because unneedy *breath*
        delicate as the sparrow's cough
    subtle as the earthworm trail

call me cassie or cassie's dream
        but hold me close the style
    of language is indirect

sign for a sign
sound for another sound

III.ix

For Zbigniew Herbert

Rilke!
        to have memorized you in German
    each dawn before driving to work

in a hot Washington office
        was what kept me sane
    for the unending phone calls

yet somehow I was never able
        to have any dialogue
    with you and your princesses

not even (as I had imagined)
        coming south through the Reschenpass
    to stay at Brunnenburg with Mary

who was also a *principessa*
            made any difference I wished
        you to be my guide

but what has life to do with wishing?
            the chance passion flower
        took over our back garden

threatened to crush our garage
            while the planted plum tree withered
        What you wrote was right

your prophetic *I am sick*
            to death of Paris
        city of the damned

in the old days an angel
            interpreted their torments
        Now I must explain them to myself   *Rilke '82 xxxvi*

against Stevens *a world*
            of poetry indistinguishable
        from the world in which we live   *Stevens 31*

yet something (perhaps Europe
            a difference of class
        or age) had intervened

I found I could not take up
            those nineteenth century
        emphases on self

Rodin's gaze restricted
            to the artistic object
        not the small girl in the garden

Rilke calling his mother
            empty as a dress
        his *wallpaper door to the world*   *Rilke-Salome 143* (4/15/04)

90

though my own
          read Rilke over and over
     underlining as she did her Nietzsche

live dangerously
               Count every day lost
     that you have not danced

I thought the gap was Europe
          until the passage
     from my northern frontier

to Poland
          where the word *culture*
     was an exotic implant

like *the intelligentsia*
          the nation-wide
     chodź kulturalnie!   *drive culturally!*

ad campaign on billboards
          and every writer
     was only too conversant

with the narrow constraints
          of history past and present
     while *out in the garden*   *Herbert '68 97*

(why have I been writing about flowers?)   *Herbert '68 59*
          aware of the corpse carried off
     the irreconcilable nature

of the aesthetic and social worlds   *Habermas 10*
          against Stevens who still believed
     in *progress* as *a general*   *Stevens 58*

transition to reality   *Stevens 23*
          (our position is that the poet
     must get rid of the hieratic

in everything that concerns him)   *Stevens 58*
   their very lack of opportunity
  giving them an edge

compelling them to stringency
   I not only envied
  but tried to cmulate

to sound like a prisoner
   since as you justly said
  Denmark is a prison   *Herbert '68 99*

coming to see more clearly
   we are all prisoners
  what we love is what we owe

and even Rilke was moved to ask
   in the midst of war
  Can art heal wounds?

Can it take the bitterness from death   *Kippenberg 143*
   Why are there not two three five
  ten who will stand together

and cry out in the market place
   Enough! *and be shot down*   *Rilke Briefe 1914-21* (10/10/15)
  but returned to what is inside us

a yet unknown remnant
   without looking
  I will make an Angel out of it   *Graff 268*

some pure word *den gelben und blaun Enzian*   *the yellow and blue gentian*
   in the tree of my dream   *Rilke '82 198*
  each tulip

was a galaxy
   revolving into
  a dot of pollen

where you can see within
   one orange molecule
  the solar system

imprisoning us
   with Aragon's torn
  corpses of insurgents   *Browder 127*

and yet Denise: *the substance*
   of an art is an incarnation   *Levertov 50*
  all around us

the dance of strangers
   in splendid upsurge
  to flowers we can only imagine

from roots we can never see

III. x

For Mother Mary John and Gary Snyder (who have never met)

The steel pentangle
   at the top of Cone Mountain
  that blue Pacific morning

its sculptor waiting
   for a helicopter
  to fly it down

gleamed in the new air
   it and the curve of the ocean
  slightly inebriating us

like the terraced vineyards
   of the Villa Serbelloni
  above the richly towered lake

from which Maylie's sister
        drove off to become a nun
      the footman holding an umbrella   *Clampitt 110*

her new life so unlike ours
        also focused on the mystery
    of dailiness

baking bread on Saturdays
        smelling the freshness
    of sun-dried laundry

while you fold the sheet
        against yourself
    from the garden line

a poet
        must move constantly
    in the direction of the credible   *Stevens 58*

as Tu Fu recognized
        from the hermit Chang
    or Petrarch from his brother the Carthusian

the serious voyage
        (he that dwelleth in love
    dwelleth in God)   *I John* 4:16

is to arrive here
        a violence from within
    that protects us

from a violence without   *Stevens 36*
        the solution
    at the center we occupy

of the universe
        where order is no longer imposed
    but comprehended

to honor wildness
          the miracle
          of Jesus is himself

not what he said or did about the future   *Rumi '84 27 (425)*
          just as she would rather
          work among vegetables

(I must start with dirt)   *Snyder '90 52*
          than be an Abbess
          so memories of vastation

(realms of taboo
          energy and richness
          like the cubic miles of krill)   *Snyder '90 11*

or aleatory epiphanies
          of say dawn from a plane
          above miles of eastward-facing

eye-piercing windows
          or in the waves off Point Reyes
          the flash of silver light

the pink salmon in the osprey's
          struggling wings
          are less than the uniqueness

of where we are now
          the escaped cloud
          of steam from the tea cup

above these morning headlines
          Meteorite in Greenhouse
          or (what is a long poem

without *nobility*?)   *Stevens 35*
          Avalanche Misses Prince   *San Francisco Chronicle* 3/11/88
          around me the smell

of kitchen linoleum
          the oak cabinet's varnish
      as my fingers touch

the grouted cross
          between the red kitchen tiles
      nesting the fresh

breakfast egg

III.xi

For Frank

At the memorial service
          I read my father's words
      of his father the Archdeacon

It is one man has fallen
          It is ourselves have risen   *F.R. Scott 190*
      all the long-lost faces

from those years in Montreal
          brides and unwedded youths   *Odyssey* 11.38
      here in the old Redpath library

where I used to check out books
          as an undergraduate
      though the woman I loved

in those years
          I did not recognize today
      I cannot see beyond

the liturgical microphone
          the absence
      that is here a presence

as I think *I am grown-up*
        can I not now come back
    to this community

that still sings hymns
        as if believing them
    together? the last famous

rebels of my father's former life
        sit in the front row
    with the bemedalled Governor-

General's aide-de-camp
        a custom dating back
    to the embattled English

citadel in Quebec
        the god represented
    by his weapons alone   *Gimbutas 202*

this service more tribal
        in its rituals
    than what we could think for ourselves

as when Joan still grieving   *Joan Blake*
        the death of her artist son
    sees Frank's face now

and hears not just his words
        but his voice here
    like the voice in the silence

of my college insomnia
        as I waited to go mad
    or the nattering cartoons

of my sensory deprivation
        in the nearby labs
    where Dr. Penfield

(whom I rescued at Okęcie   *Warsaw airport*
        from the Polish UB   *secret police*
    for his undeclared złotys)

stimulated the posterior
        right temporal lobe
        "Again I hear voices"   *Jaynes 108-09*

(*Hear my words*
        on Hammurabi's stele)   *Jaynes 198*
    and where still earlier I declined

to apply the scalpel
        to the exposed breast
    her gaze still meaningful

and partly stunning
        except where one eye
        and below it the jaw's musculature

had been removed
        What does it mean
        to speak of illusion?

I had seen a towhee
        flutter into my class
    on Dante's *Paradiso*

but my reader said afterwards
        with an authority
    I had heard from no other student

Oh no, Professor Scott!
        it was a white dove!
    my father's heaven

was *the future of man*   *F.R. Scott 89*
        (where power was
    let justice be

and not *the canons of construction*)   *F.R. Scott 80*
       the human race was his race   *F.R. Scott 89*
   not the outworn privileges

of an Anglican compact
       but *supreme confidence*
   in Canada

and *individual rights*   *Djwa 394-96*
       Does one now say *Naive!*
   when in the *crise d'Octobre*

my father's respect for law
       respected the emergency arrests
   under the War Measures Act?   *Djwa 409*

and even his civil rights victories
       very much his father's son   *Djwa 317*
   are now said to have been eroded?

Or is it not still as it was
       that truth and justice exist
   (even speaking to us

as Osiris *true-of-voice*   *Jaynes 189*
       the Sibyl under the goad
   of relentless Apollo

or Penfield's epileptic
       Sylvère Sylvère)   *Jaynes 110*
   and yet we live by lies?

Again I hear voices   *Jaynes 109*
       the advice of Pythagoras
   to the well-meaning legislator

that *all things change*   *Ovid Met. 15.165*
       Last night unfathered
   I could almost not sleep

I felt so criminally alive
            I have just seen
      my dearest friend from those days

and did not recognize her
            this cross-implanted mountain
      and its white river

dwarfed by new high-rises
            the riot-proof Le Penfield
      On the wooded north side

four Scott generations
            still buried beneath one oak
      amid the fallen headstones

of the Godfreys and the Bethunes
            wrecked in the tide
      of youths from the parade

of the St. Jean Baptiste Society
      the betrayal
      of Laurendeau's dream   *Djwa 401*

just as all pride of stone
            will surely pass
      In the Ross Pavilion   *Royal Victoria Hospital*

still reiterating
      the idea of equal partnership   *Djwa 425*
      my father himself saw

a tyger come through the door
      a t-y-g-e-r
      prowled round the hospital bed

and was about to leap at me
his paws already in the air
when I fixed my eyes on his

and blasted him to hell

III. xii

For Betty Anne Affleck

And if I write last of you
        it is because you were first
    and those stirrings so deep

not your name nor seeing you again
        can help me remember
    even though what we searched for

we never quite attained
        like the post-war commonwealth
    our clean politics never came close to achieving

and if I forgot you first
        it is because you fit
    least into what followed

I wonder *Is there*
        in every so-called civilized male life
    some Dido on that far shore

driving us like Pound into ever
        more unnatural projects
    and more inaccessible language

heavy with her weight
        yet by our sweet delay
    among the first cherry blossoms

Pound Canto 7/27

the fox cubs cuffing at creekside
        that nippy April in the cedars
   even after two years

those unnegotiated restraints
        our first and only night together
   in the Vermont boathouse

the steam of our frightened breath
        and the steam of the lilied pond
   you softened me

from the bitterness of my asceticism
        and spared me the bitterness of license
   and if we were slow to discover

the face of death that waits
        behind all things even love
    (Ist sie den Liebenden leichter?   *Is it easier for lovers?*

Ach, sie verdecken sich   *Alas, they merely conceal*
        nur mit einander ihr Los)   *with each other their own fate*
   life is long why hurry that?   *Rilke '82 150*

and if in hindsight
        we were as old-fashioned
   as we considered our parents

having still known the fear
        of *what people might think*
   (with no conception

of the bliss actually conveyed
        by the noise of our nightly scufflings
   on that too narrow stairwell

to the artistic imaginations
        of Eldon and Betty downstairs
   and from them even to my mother)

is this nostalgia for awe
          bashfulness fear?
     how without them to have known that sweetness?

dare I say this to my student
          who corrected me *No!*
     each first kiss is a nightmare!

my other student who tells me
          of the cult she heard of
     through the California School of Art

where the women are breeders
          breeders that is of children
     for the sacrifices?

there is time for all good things
          let them still be slow as we were
     let me retain that sureness

that could hear *this love*
          is older and better than you are
     this joy you experience

augments the world's joy
          in its creating
     and since morals change

since art has sung so much of liberation
          let it still praise the restraints
     the body's code composes

with the support of a world
          come to peace with itself
     so there can still be sweetness

even in excesses
          which would have shocked us then
     which shocked me decades later

even in the tired face
of the young woman on the beach
being fucked slowly one more time

(while others are oiling themselves
play energetic Frisbee
or read the Entertainment Section

of the *San Francisco Chronicle*
and while at the farthest cliffs
there are other wilder sports

demonism
the endless freedom of the will
to remake the world   *Fekete xvii*

I have no wish to write about)
the young man you can tell
is truly her lover

knows her as only a lover can
by the smile that bares her teeth
as slowly silently

in that absented gaze
she may sometime reach again
in pregnancy

her head nods yes

III.xiii

For the children

Sitting together
for the first time in the months
since Maylie became a priest

on the windowsill
               the portions of honeycomb
          gnawed away by mice

that Cassie our plumber
               pulled out from inside the wall
          behind the bathtub

so many bees
               just when the children were leaving
          no one minded occasional stings

in the bee-heavy garden
               under the passion vine
          but the threat that so many

hundred pounds of sweetness
               might seep through the wall
          and ruin the dining room

made us bring in Hal
               the Berkeley pacifist
          amateur bee-tender

with his elaborate stratagem
               to divert the bees
          to his portable hive

and unseal the wall
               for new hordes of robber bees
          so many of whom died anyway

not finding his exit hole
               they would crawl up my left leg
          for electrifying bee za-zen

the house empty now
               and the world still as adverse
          as when Yeats with *bees*

in his *loosening masonry*   *Yeats CP 204*
            mused on *that senseless tumult*   *Yeats CP 206*
        of *those who labour from hatred*   *Yeats CP 461*

(the word *senseless*
            an excuse for limited vision?
        the nun: "What do you do

when even to help the orphans
            is considered an act of subversion?"   *Herman and Chomsky 351*
        her underpants in her mouth   *Herman and Chomsky 62*

a *victim of mindless violence*
            according to *Time*   *Time* 12/15/80;
        ignoring the radio intercepts   *Herman and Chomsky 63*

two witnesses "missing in action"
            two judges resigning in fear)   *Herman and Chomsky 65-67*
        in such a time it is still good

having danced until midnight
            to Mika's and John's new band
        after the family lasagna

all generations
            our children and their friends
        dancing together singly

to be back in that silence
            behind the self that clown
        just now in the bathroom mirror

behind the masks
            of deliberate mythologies
        (from old words we should gather

only this silence they have defined
            a lake reflecting flowers   *Baller 74*
        moonlight free from possessiveness)   *Pound Canto 99/703*

the *radical innocence*
        of that mindlessness
      when we turn from past injuries

towards the future
        (the true future not mere foresight
      extrapolating the present)

from that sweet disturbance
        where if teeth have darkened flesh
      and the abandonment

of one couple to happiness
        has left others in suffering
      there is still the return

to this breathing za-zen
        a form of procreation
      the last word always to the children

and for us former children
        no longer even parents
      this faint smell of beeswax

the broken honeycombs
        no longer cloying
      but empty

hexagons

IV

My fame need only belong to the north hall
                                                    —Ikkyu

IV.i

For James Schamus and Nancy Kricorian

My grandfather among
        the yellow water lilies
    the pitcher plant

restrain your own spirit
        why, Tiresias?
        (my heart is an inkjar ⚱

I have come at the wish of my heart
        from the pool of double Fire)   *Budge 25*
    the first FIELD

my mother painted in the forties
        was formal but dab by dab
    the heavy impasto returned

on the sand–flecked open–
        handed aborigine
    you can see through (plus red)

not only the earlier
        senses of "form" rejected
    but equally "subject"

as a conceptual focus
          has given place to the literal
          activity of writing itself   *Creeley '73 259*

(losing even that sense
          of something lost
to be recuperated?)

old pre-war
          Winsor and Newton pigments
          indigo rose madder

not to reach a conclusion
          but to keep our exposure
          to what we do not know   *Duncan '66 224*

veridian green
          replaced by new free-flowing
          ether-based acrylics

in the States the color-fields
          of Pollock and Sam Francis
          perception to perception   *Olson 149*

Alfred Kazin reproving Pound
          for ignoring the quotidian
          always his pre-war cafés

of the Paris literati
          semina motuum
          a poetic politics

to replace the lyrical subject
          never once Pennsylvania
          COMPOSITION BY FIELD

split second acts   *Olson 149*
          consciousness of forms
          not to refine

but to shatter them
       the grands récits
    dispersed into clouds

of linguistic particles   *Lyotard 8; Foster 64*
       But *an entire*
    effacement of the self

and restitution of the stylus   *Kuberski 48*
      is this possible?   *P.D. Scott '86A 71*
    The pigments of Sam Francis

run heavily down the sides
      the center is white
    (language without syntax

immediacy: Osiris
      before he was torn apart)   *Perelman 23*
    for myself at the margins

of my once institutional life
      the week behind the fluttering
    red flag of the chauffeured

ambassadorial Buick
      Basha the terrorizable
    peasant Polish maid

with the oldest of dialects
      (Tse'gihi
    House made of dark mist

House made of female rain
      house made of pollen
    house made of grasshoppers

dark cloud is at the door   *Kinnell 236*
      Orpingalik calling this song
    "my breath" because [he said]

"it is just as necessary
for me to sing
as it is to breathe")   Rothenberg 226, 563

who forgot my breakfast
          while I lay in the ambassador's bed
     rereading the *Gorgias*

I was about to teach freshmen
          τῇ ὡς ἀληθῶς πολιτικῇ τεχνῇ
     the true art of politics   Gorgias 521D

which led to Arnold quoting
          from Joubert *force*
     till right is ready

till right is ready, force   Perelman 15
          and afterwards funds from the California
     Council on the Arts

to "critique" (smash)
          the bourgeois interior decorator
     acting out his fantasy

of pre-market wholeness
          The sky is leaded with elm boughs   Perelman 24
     and for Fanny whose first husband

the one with a stockbroker's name
          came to dinner late
     with his female lab assistant

the intention of Paradise
          could be liberationist
     if it didn't deny

the possibility
          of a project
     larger than its language   Howe 134

114

next to the impasto
       of burnt sienna Prussian blue
    the unsized canvas

white of the quotidian
       tideflow under the sun
    the mothering swell and ebb

If you look you will see the salamander   Duncan '66 213
       and yet *to indulge myself*
    in pretentious fictions

this art in search of itself   Duncan '54 185-86
       the freedom to quote
    even from emperors

and not to be called *exactly wrong*   Perelman 25
       after the praise
    of *the form-creator*

which compels the ovule to evolve   Perelman 17
       (less danger in hateful
    than in seductive myth

the seeds of movement)   Pound Canto 80/500
       to dismantle
    while others still erect

the scaffolding of discourse   Bernstein 31
       and to heal past error
    mastering what was

opening out upon what must be   Duncan '66 224
       and accident! thinking
    at first the ice

of the small alpine lake
       firm enough to walk on
    (give to me my mouth

may I follow my heart
          at its season of fire and night)   *Budge 26*
     then breakthrough! our legs

as frigid as someone else's
          the maternal concept
          of reality here emerging

is immediately dreadful   *Marcuse 230*
          a quick plunge and out
     to the hot steep bank

of cadmium yellow
          avalanche lilies
          (not a phrase

of our communication
          that is meaningless)   *Duncan '66 218*
     each burning its halo

(O flames! O reservoirs!)
through the snow

IV.ii

For Raquel Scherr and Leonard Michaels

Just off the coast trail
          one naked woman in half-lotus
     ablaze in the setting sun

like a nostalgic poster
          for the 1960s
     those dreams beyond power

having entered the Foreign Service
          and nine days later
     the government fell

I now joined the English Department
        and six months after
        my first course on Dante

aestas amoris
                the Summer of Love
        dancing in the Polo Grounds

with Carol on my shoulders
        and Mika on hers
        the summer of love and tear gas

they body-painted Cassie
                Allen chanted Blake
        on a platform with Hell's Angels

at *The Gathering of the Tribes*
                planned by Sherman Kent's brother-in-law
        who possessed a tarot deck

with the handwritten annotations
                of the infamous Aleister Crowley
        to psychedelicize the radical left   *Lee 157-58*

while Jolly West my UC colleague   *Louis Jolyon West*
        editor of the text
        reporting my *hallucinations*   *West 88*

(*like Wordsworth Eliot*
                uses emotion *for* arousal
        and his objective correlative

seems analogous
                to our cortical interpretation)   *Siegel and West 198*
        who gave 300,000 mikes

of CIA acid to an elephant
                in MK-Ultra research   *Lee 48; Marks 59*
        to duplicate "rut" madness

but the animal just keeled over
        in a motionless stupor   *Lee 22*
   and who when Jack Ruby

began to talk in jail
        of a *right-wing conspiracy*
       found Jack was *paranoid*   *Lee 189*

Jolly West *rented a pad*
        in the heart of Haight-Ashbury
   to study *the hippies*

in their native habitat   *Lee 190*
        with demonstrations of joy
   singing and dancing

shaking the body
        saying Ha, Ha, Ha!
   long poles with feathers on the end

this being their sign of peace   *Font 366-68*
        while Hitchcock's chemist Owsley
   gave away STP

which had just been tested
        at the Edgewood Arsenal   *Lee 187*
   I too *in that dawn*

was glad to become alive
        though I soon could see
   that the sweet *insegnamento*

of Dante's erotic friendships
        had made few converts among my students
   and feared that so much innocence

they live with anyone they desire
        and leave them whenever they please   *Font 97-122*
   would soon lead to so much rape

others stopped in rainbow mind
        to this very day
    having donated their bodies

without regard to the Platonic
        notion of the soul
    making the *great refusal*   *Marcuse 149*

When the beautiful
        witch in my epic class
    took me to a coven

not sky-clad but wearing
        my dusty sixties psychedelics
    I heard the Yeatsian

druidism of the *fin-de-siècle*
        which the rogue Crowley
    brought to the Bay Area

the Satanic Masses
        over naked female bodies
    the freethinker Max Scherr

used to publish in the *Barb*
        Was Pound a male witch?
    Eleusis no more than a cover

for authoritarian indulgences?
        Baker Roshi's fashionable mix
    of Stevens and Bodhidharma

more than a Harvard ego's
        taking advantage of
    our historic need

to reinvent the primitive?
        these local dreamers
    a constant recrudescence

of local authoritarianism   *Du Bois 498*
        And now Laura tells me   *Laura Nader*
    it was not the students

who asked for sexual permissiveness
       it was the deans!
They wanted our innocence

the *Gathering of the Tribes*
      who had been hunted
like wild beasts lassoed

and forced into slavery   *Heizer '79 2*
      oak trees fenced in
the acorns needed for hogs   *Heizer '79 130*

accusation of stolen stock
      no concept of private ownership
at dawn men in ambush

would shoot every Indian that appeared
      Indian evidence not
admissible in a court of justice   *Heizer '79 128*

(the newspapers then
      an enlightened nation
has raised her flag   *Heizer '74 5*

We are opposed to mob law
      but have ever approved
of Vigilance Committees

of respectable citizens   *Heizer '74 50*
      like the newspapers now)
the Indians relocated to the Sierra

snow from October to June
      even a Special Agent
from the Atlantic Littoral

ought to have known better   *Heizer '79 132*
        Rexroth Lowell Larkin
        all in a sense male witches

an old Mohave woman
        searches for pine nuts
        while the Rome plows

flatten the piñon pines
        and we keep peace
        as people scrambled

to gather the food
        a government helicopter
        fired down on them

a man lying on a cot
        inside a church
        was hit by a bullet

when his wife accompanied him
        to a hospital
        she was arrested and jailed   *Zinn 524*

the expense for relief
a single drydock costs twice that   *Heizer '79 3*

                        IV.iii

            For Stephen Greenblatt

But I too was tribal
        when as a young bureaucrat
        I moved through the corridors of power

and learned that advancement
        was achieved by avoiding
        certain walls of silence

still more by the profession
            of a certain worldliness
        the words of Aeneas

(having let *the wife*
            follow in his footsteps
        at a proper distance)   *longe servet vestigia coniunx* Aen. 2.711

durate, et vosmet   *endure and save yourselves*
            rebus servate secundis   *for things to come Aen. 1.207*
        or in that particular spring

the concern of our NATO allies
            especially Portugal
        as the bureaucratic knives

having to *dispense*
            with all sentimentality   *FRUS '48 1.2.524-25; Chomsky 48*
        such as equality of race

swiftly dismembered the Charter
            Diefenbaker had commissioned
        from Northrop Frye on human rights

those hard exteriors for promotion
            racked with deep despair   *Paradise Lost 1.126; Aen. 1.208-09*
        it might seem that heroism

is for those who do not think
            and I have heard *culture*
        defined as precisely

that servile part in all of us
            which we imitate
        from our environment

but can it be otherwise?
            the more we choose and reject
        the more we become

is it so different
        with today's postmodern poets
        reading Foucault or the *APR*   *American Poetry Review*

as assiduously as brokers
        scan stock market reports
        even you the best of our critics

who see how the Renaissance
        principle of negation
        tore the *self* from the *communal body*   *Greenblatt '80 159*

how *any achieved identity*
        contains within itself
        the signs of its own subversion   *Greenblatt '80 9*

as you pick apart Spenser's
        near-tragic sense of the cost
        of *"civility"* achieved

through renunciation and power   *Greenblatt '80 173*
        you then speak of Virgil's
        celebration of power

adoration of Augustus   *Greenblatt '80 174*
        as if every epic
        author were like Spenser

an agent and apologist of massacre   *Greenblatt '80 186*
        (whose Una says *spoile her*   *F.Q.* 1.8.45
        as did Grey's predecessor Pelham

Repair into Kerrie
        and prey burn spoil and destroy)   *Carew MSS II.307*
        with a guilty conscience

they loked like Anotomies of deathe
        they did eat the dead carrions
        any stony heart

would have rued the same   *Spenser Vewe 3259-62; F.Q. 1.8.41*
      while Virgil himself
   whatever Dante thought

of the *good Augustus*   *Inf.* 1.71
      in *low-lying Italy*   *umile Italia Inf.* 1.106; *Aen.* 3.522-23
   wrote of *the gifts of nations*   *dona populorum*

Augustus had hung
      on the *proud doors of Phoebus*   *Phoebi superbis postibus*
   as the doors of Priam before him   *postes superbi*
Aen. 8.720-22; 2.504

had been *hung with barbaric gold*
      in *haughty Troy*   *superbo Ilion Inf.* 1.75; *Aen.* 3.2-3
   To prosper at words (themselves

a form of commerce) is to outdo
      in conventions established
   by repetition

the halls of this English Department
      have their own vocabulary
   phallocentric or *police*

to replace *icon*
      irony mythopoeia
   and for those on the margin

openness field or space)
      can powerful bureaucracies
   share more than cynicism

conspiring from whichever
      viewpoint to subordinate
   culture to policy

by *the power of the state*
      to contain *apparently subversive gestures*
   or even to produce *them*   *Montrose 21; Greenblatt '88*

suppressing *doubleness*
       (not *the sites of institutional*
       and ideological contestation   *Montrose 34; Greenblatt '88 2-3*

a *set of manipulations*   *Greenblatt '89 12*
       in *the cultural system of meanings*
       that creates specific individuals   *Greenblatt '80 3-4; Pecora 267*

every last one of them
       cultural artifacts)   *Geertz 51; Pecora 267; Scott '89 119*
       by doubleness I mean

the power within us
       by inspiration
       or *the return of the repressed*

to answer itself
       shell shielding softness
       new moon holding full

one shepherd lamenting
       the irreparable loss
       of all most dear *vernichtet*

by the latest experts
       in rural pacification
       the other against all evidence

empowering what we are not
       singing of peace
       mitescent saecula aspera

the hard ages will soften   *Aen.* 1.291

IV.iv

For LuEllen Schafer

History as a parade
        the people coming up the street
     Chicano banners *fuero fuero*

nostalgic white-haired Longshoremen
        joyous-fisted lesbians
     the Faculty Peace Committee

closely drilled Black Panthers
        sedate Friends with baby-carriages
     Suburban Mothers of Gays

and before all that ended
        the sexual rituals
     of Black Flag Communes

yeilding to bullets and burning police cars
        (it is necessary to look exhaustively
     into the negative and demonic)   *Snyder '68* 115

there was free food in the Polo Grounds
        from Diggers who proclaimed
     the age of free giving had returned

the chance to start fresh
        (the stranger I caught sight of
     in the men's room mirror

wearing what seemed to be my clothes)
        always at hand
     making me ask in turn

to what in the end
        did I ever make
     this most precious gift

my only life?
        we thought at first
        our experimental college

would change the world
            no less than the idea
        a few faculty and students together

study precisely what we wanted
            which may have meant
        being more timely than we thought

rejoicing in *togetherness*
            process self-criticism
        the Great Subculture

which runs underground
            not *accomplices of the State*   *Snyder '68 114-15*
        that day at the vineyard

nakedness still in fashion
            all ages we leapt
        into the lake like lemmings

and a few of us swam
            to the other side
        which jutted out like an island

we stood there for ten minutes
            breathing silently as if the world
        were on the edge of a millennium

as to whether we changed
            I can say this
        just when I lacked it

you were *a force: the rarest thing*   *Tsvetaeva to Rilke*
            to draw me outside the frail
        elaborate construct

of my professional career
            and taught me my pleasure
        was neither anarchy

so soon brutal
            nor civilization
        surpassing it in brutality

but the instruction of play
            decorum instead of law
        instead of custom   dance

your feet effortlessly
off the ground

IV.v

For Czeslaw Milosz

An old man contemptuous blackhearted
            dumbfounded that such a short time ago
        he was twenty

challenges my English self
            I am reading in bed
        the reason Denise was glad

to be single once again
            the Polish I once breathed
        Stary człowiek wzgardliwy

kochał i pragnał
            but it turned out badly
        the world was faster than he was

and now he sees the illusion   *Milosz '84 18-19*
            we are past midsummer
        the song sparrow rarely sings

Maylie away again
       the goldfinch shakes the wire
   coming up under our eave

as the fog wanders through the elms
      while he high above us
   looks out like Issa or Wang Wei

through the dripping redwoods   *Milosz '84 206*
      on this sea of white fog
   with sirens in it

Słyszę twój śmiech w ogrodzie
      I hear your laughter in the garden   *Milosz '84 124-25*
   could that have been my English

his Polish eye gleaming
      when after search for a phrase
   the shortcomings of our two tongues

shaping an aporia
      and to plug this blacked-out space
   some new word-shape worked

as if the universe
      had given birth to an atom
   and we knew we were pleased with our invention

and with language itself
      potential messenger
   to a few good people   *Milosz '84 192*

before he turned on me
      my not reflecting
   how cruel nature is, and so on   *Merton 139*

it was he who taught me
      what was to be preserved
   in the abandonment of cities

was it by some
               failure or transgression
        I had to forfeit

that inebriation of language
               or were we too similar
        I thought having arrived

at the solitude of one's fifties
               a poet would no longer care
        if we had been for the winning

or losing cause in Vietnam
               when desires for a stranger
        who happens to stoop

for a pencil on the carpet
               or the surge when crowded against
        the teenage siren

in a two-piece bathing-suit
               her wet hair dripping chlorine
        on the hotel elevator floor

have become as if memories
               as bizarre and alien
        as quaggas at the city zoo

(What are we if not wanting
               when we grope for desire and find
        only contentment?)

I thought that having exhausted
               the furor of those barricades
        and arrived at the preparation of sauces   *Milosz '84 200-01*

we would turn in gratitude
               to the clear speech of poets
        the cares of old angers

dim as the flattened
            world so far below
        I wrote to say this

and got back his great Polish chuckle
            my dear Peter of course
        you gave the enemy comfort

you cannot compare
            a lemon with a triangle   *Milosz '86 34*
        this fragile culture

and all its faults
            with that which is a cancer
        I miss you you inveterate warrior

waging the last peace
            so much the maker of your world
        there is hardly room in it

for the voices of the young
            and writing out of your fierce heart
        precisely because there is no one

else left like you
            (Should I really experience
        nature as alien

and heartless?   *Merton 139*
            as you would have me do
        I read *Commentary*

the young Vietnamese student
            who like yourself stayed on
        after the revolution

All of us could see
            the brutality of Saigon
        the other side remained hidden)   *Doan 43*

We are divided
          by our separate gratitudes
     each wanting to atone

for years of well-meaning service
          with opposing governments
     in the name of peace

Can the poet Issa replace
          the valley of your childhood
     in which places and people have disappeared?

For you *everything grows smaller*   *wszystko zgęszcza się*
          meaning in turn that you   *Milosz '84 198-99*
     must grow smaller to me

though no less noble
          and what is poetry
     if not the salvation of a people?

an inner elixir?
          language's blind erasure
     of its human origins?

or a pair of jade discs? Can these surpass
          two men ploughing the southern fields   *Wang Wei 198*
     while the empire surges?   *Confucius Analects 18.6*

Her *sesshin* how long?   *retreat*
          Congress voting again tomorrow
     my mother busy

arranging about the books
          that were once my father's
     With whom if not humans

am I to associate?
          I cannot associate with birds   *Confucius Analects 18.6*
     I recite in bed

132

to the muttering windowshades
in my empty bedroom
I wszędzie tutaj

przemawiają głosy
And on all sides voices
in such great numbers   Milosz '84 20-21

the smooth circle
on the back of my wrist
where my watch

is missing

IV.vi

For Ron and Gillian Graham

To my right a row of monks
and once again to my left
a wall this one of paper

the stream flowing
broken waterfall of birds
soon we will chant

shiki soku ze ku   *form namely emptiness*
my mind lifts
bushwhack up creekbed

past pour of water
from shallow *oriyoki* pool
to the Ventana South Cone

the silent mountain lion
staring for a moment
and disappearing across the trail

high above white clouds
　　　　before the great cedars
　　were burnt in the fire

to the sound *namo*　　　　　　　　　　　　　　　南無　*hail! I submit*
　　　　Maylie repeated sewing
　　each stitch in her robe

she will soon be ordained
　　　　Baker Roshi gone now
　　I copied the Chinese

on the deck by the dry creek
　　　　of the small library
　　behind the zen-do

not as I imagined
　　　　nan² wu² south without　南無
　　as in Annam　安南 or Vietnam　　走南

but eighth century *na³ mo²*　南無
　　　　as Sangyo heard it
　　I take refuge in

or even older
　　　　I submit to
　　the Monier-Williams

Dictionary of Sanskrit
　　　　next to my Mathews
　　gives the oldest meaning

　　नम् *nam to bend or bow*
　　　　(Siddhartha's *nanta*)
　　subject or submit oneself

Hari om namo Shivaye　　　　　　　　　　　　*Hail to Shiva*
　　　　on Allen's postcard about drugs　　　　*Ginsberg 95*
　　the nine prostrations

134

we shall shortly perform
      the Gandharan Buddha again the same
   after eleven centuries

the disastrous grease-fire
      which spread from the kitchen)
   and citing *νέμεσις*   *nemesis*

the epic hang-up
      we once mystified as Fate
   and now see historically

as human resentment
      take in your hearts
   each man of you

αἰδῶ καὶ νέμεσιν   *aidō kai nemesin*
      shame and indignation   *Iliad* 13.122
   or Odysseus' boast-word

you had no fears
      of the indignation of men   *Odyssey* 22.40
   I hear the whack

of the *jun-ko*'s ruler   *order-keeper*
      keeping our spines near-straight
   our heads even mine near-empty

νέμος and *nemus*   *nemos*
      the sacred grove
   from the act of dispensing

and then pasture or feed
      why last of the flock
   ever far the first

νέμεαι τέρεν' ἄνθεα   *nemeai teren' anthea*
      to feed on the tender grass   *Odyssey* 9.449
   it had taken so long

for us to talk together
      not about him
    my mother saying first

from the ward desk telephone
      two days or seven weeks
    and then *I walked by*

acacia flowers in the gutter
      and despite what people think
    knew I could still be happy

and Anglo-Saxon *niman*
      seize carry off
    Ne nom he in þæm wicum

nor seized he from that hall
      so old is the word of power   *Beowulf* 1612
    against our wishes

shrinking in modern English
      like *gylp* to *yelp*   *boast honorably*
    nim now *only archaic*   *steal (17th Cy)*

and *naam* in the law schools)   *goods taken in distraint*
      there! the bell hum
    hanging outside like smoke

in the narrow canyon
      the sun has begun to enter
    the thock of the *han*   *wooden gong*

we shall rise soon
      to the diminutive *nimble*
    the deprived *numb*

as in Wordsworth's
      My hands are numb   *Borderers* 727
    making murder possible

but not the restoration of the world
        and Rilke's *so leben wir*
   und nehmen immer Abschied

so we live
and forever take our leave
Rilke '82 196

my perverse knees
        the fading residue
    above the stream

for a moment
        silence
    that cannot be transcribed

wishing and submission
        like music Stravinsky
   our innermost point

as the other side of the air
        no longer habitable
    in a community

Rilke '82 146

of pure impulse
there would be only Names

Námas

IV. vii

For Mary de Rachewiltz

Lineages! the last
        satisfaction of our desire
    for the vertical

the thought that Dante
        might have inhaled from Cunizza
    as an old woman

in the Cavalcanti household
the creative whatever-it-is urge
of *Eleanor jauzionda*'s

secrets of Montségur
Maylie's new lineage
through Dogen and Bodhidharma

and having myself once talked
a few minutes with Gilbert Murray
ninety-five years old

by a hedgerow on Boar's Hill
I imagined falsely
that he might have heard

from Lady Rosamond
what Trevelyan knew of Shelley
not knowing his childhood

in New South Wales
his father gazetted
with the Mounted Police

to suppress bush-ranging
his cousin the Gilbert
of the *Bab Ballads*

provincials like myself
or Pound who had hoped to hear
Swinburne mimic Landor

We need these myths
Virginia Woolf imagining
she had been deprived

when she could not at Cambridge
join the Apostles
the only one of that crew

spared for a vocation
        having to self-invent
   or Mary returning

from mowing the Alpine meadows
        to excitement in Gais
   the carabinieri arrested

Mamme at the corner of the house   *de Rachewiltz 184*
      Do Hearr kemm   *The gentleman has come*
   the man out of Italy

for whom the saddler had made
        a couch in the living room   *de Rachewiltz 27*
   Thy truth then be thy dower

this precisely the gift
        Nulla per me io desidero   *For me nothing But that life*
   che la vita continui cosi   *continue like this   de Rachewiltz 151*

the rest nothing
        that the legal heir should marry
   my child-bride Elizabeth Parkin

that my aunt should discover
        behind the parish church
   for nearly six centuries

the manor descended
        through the Flemings of Wath
   to Thomas Norris   *Earl 6*

the lichened slab
        of Elizabeth Norris Dale
   whose granddaughter-in-law

would model the hand
        holding high the famed decrepit
   torch of liberty

as if saying *Forget*
               your ancestors
To May Sarton (as to myself)

We were given much
               the great year
of medieval history

with Anne Thorp in Grade VII
               a granddaughter of Longfellow   *Sarton 115, 117-18*
but those students who went on

to Phillips Exeter and Harvard
               or stayed close to their salt
family graveyards

had less of a chance
               than did my grandmother
who from Cacouna recalled

the Maxwells of Munches
               and indeed was descended
from fabled Eleanor

if not *Sigifredo*
               so much history flung
in one's face smelling of earth   *de Rachewiltz 269*

but whose chief profit
               from so much family disgrace
was the shame

which made her like so many
               flee to Canada
More space! more mornings

watching the sunlight descend
               the east flanks of the Inyos
to the saline desert

the air on the brow
      of the two companions
     with the force of a gentle breeze   *Purg.* 28.7-9

and with what Galtung
      after meeting his young wife
     in the Tokyo airport

with a sign up GALTUNG!
      called *entropy*
     that state of grace

when the words are free
to write themselves

IV.viii

For Robert Pinsky and Frank Bidart

We rise in our plane
      like post-Romantics
     pulling away from our shadow

on the subjected plain
      (though the two-dimensional
     incoherence of language

still calls us the *subject*)
      no other way
     than to have worked through all this

to have dealt with the other voice
      that refuses *No! No!*
     it has to be more work

there is something unreal
      about 'inhabiting
   a cloud'

yet *this is it* the experience
      so long ago in Dante
   that the impulsive imagination

can swoop down like a hawk
      on anyone *I will pour out*
   my spirit on all flesh

this faculty in all   *ben Maimon* 2.33–38
      despite all odds
   and personal experience

pressing us to believe
      in the conversion
   of love itself

writing not on and on
      from beginning to end
   like Milton dictating blindly

to reluctant daughters
      but backwards and forwards
   either end a beginning

the lines of Komachi:
      the world wrongs us
   because of Paradise   *Merton* 252–53

mind returning on itself
      a concentration
   which does not happen consciously

or of deliberation   *Eliot '32 21*
      as if Dante
   breaking inwards like a thief

non stringer ma rallarga   *Purg.* 9.58
      do not restrain but open
   (and later the mountain trembled)   *Purg.* 20.127–28

142

had his image reversed
>the way gulls on a screen
>might wing backwards dropping

out of their fierce beaks
>morsels of white bread
>into my gesticulating

thumb and fingers working
>the well–fitted pieces
>into a loaf

not just in the prosaic
>reversal that it was his
>talent brought the hawk down

into his poem but his more mystic
>being *rapt up to the fire*
>to write his own voice

this writing upon writing
>*trucks and helicopters*
>*on the surface of Olympia*

the Rokeby Venus
>*with pictures of mosquitoes and a truck)*   *Foster 47, 53*
>a *scraped-again*

palimpsest
>much less *impasto*
>than archaeology or excoriation

mining the lithographic stone
>again and again
>for what was not within it

by removal of the unwanted
>the unrecognized on return
>this excavation

of the unlimited future
        disclosing the geology
        of the original heart   本心 pen³ hsin¹ *Mencius* 6A:10.8;
                                                                Bodhidharma 8

a love so vast
        as in the long run
        to prove intolerable

the inscriptions and reinscriptions
        of culture corrupt
        with the *purer eye of intention*   *Thomas à Kempis* 3.33.2

but accepting the task
        not to express
        the personal *I have forgotten my umbrella*   *Foster 99*

but to communicate
        what can be received
        (he excavated

this astonishing darkness
        not from the brazen plate
        but from the living rock

of some subterranean world)   *Stevens 48-49*
        even the debt I feel
        to Maylie's vocation

which as we move out beyond
        the fulfilment of marriage
        gives us each the space

to sit as I do now
        in this plane coming down
        over the fields of Mexico

to rejoin its shadow
             this vacancy distance
    of separation

we can only call a *gift*

IV.ix

For Brendan O Hehir and Laura Morland-O Hehir

I am what I wish

the Sanskrit   **काम**   kā́ma
pleasure enjoyment
especially sexual
a stake in gambling
a species of mango tree
a meter of four lines
a kind of bean
a particular form of temple
semen virile

the Javanese ꦏꦩ ꦫ   kâma
desire passion semen
the Old Javanese   kâmamohita
drunk with love
             kâmabâna arrow of desire
             Sakâma-kâma all manner of desires
the Old Persian   kamana
loving true faithful
the Persian   کام   kám
the Turkish   kam
the Irish   caomh
dear handsome gentle
(the English *comely*)
             caomhnaigh cherish
             caomhnaí companion

the Sanskrit   *kamala*
lustful
dry and sterile soil
a form of jaundice

the Yurok *skewok*
to want to wish to love
skewo$^{?}$ to be generous
skewi$^{?}$r to be smooth
(trees, etc.)
skewip- to be well shaped
ske$^{?}$woy- to be ripe to be cooked
skewo$^{?}$m to smell good

the Chinese 欲   *yü^4*
wish desire
On the point of
    姪欲   *yin^2 yü^4* sexual desire
    欲海   *yü^4 hai^3* the sea of desire
    慾海   *yü^4 hai^3* the sea of passion
    天欲雨   *t'ien^1 yü^4 yü^4*
it is about to rain
    欲不欲 *yü^4 pu^4 yü^4* (Taoist)
to desire
the absence of desire

the Latin *volo*
to wish will
mean endeavor
the English *weal*
I will and *it will*
we are men of velleity   *Merton 331*
the English *wealth*

St. Augustine
nam non solum ire
verum etiam pervenire illuc

nihil erat aliud
quam velle ire
for not only to go
but even to arrive there
was nothing other
than to wish to go   *Conf. 8.8.12*

Borduas *les tableaux*   *the paintings*
sur lesquels ma volonté   *which my will*
s'acharne le plus   *is the most eager*
à vouloir diriger   *to wish to direct*
sont ceux qui deviennent   *are those which become*
les plus lointains   *the most distant*
J'achète le décapitant   *I buy paint remover*   *Borduas 88*

and Eliot
the extinction of personality   *Eliot '32 17*
before receiving

ṭaṭa àb

what the heart hands you

                    IV.x

    For Svetlana Alpers and Paul Alpers
    (and for Calvin Tomkins scriptor)

The day that Wall Street
            fell 508 points
        van Gogh's *Irises*

painted the first week
            at the private asylum
        of Saint-Paul-de-Mausole

the sky blue
> *the sun sheds a radiance of sulphur*
it absorbs me so much

I let myself go
> *without thinking of any rules*   *Tomkins 38*
went on view in Sotheby's

for auction by its owner
> John Payson the art dealer
grandson of Payne Whitney

who explained that *Irises*
> *had become too expensive to keep*   *Tomkins 37*
Theo to Vincent

they have put it on the narrow wall of the room
> there were no buyers
but Theo was hopeful

I think we can wait patiently
> *for success to come*
you will surely live to see it

after Vincent to Theo
> *Nor do I regard your sneers*
aimed expressly at me

but you fire at the barricade
> *and I happen to be there*   *Van Gogh 312*
before he shot himself

and Theo's complete mental breakdown
> from which he never recovered
dying one month before

Mirbeau's long essay
> in *L'Echo de Paris*
and his purchase of *Irises*

for a derisory sum   *Tomkins 48*
          Monet to Mirbeau: *How*
     did a man who loved flowers and the light

manage to be so unhappy?   *Tomkins 50*
          It went in 1905
     to the collector Pellerin

whose fortune came
          from the manufacture of margarine
     to the dealer Bernhaim-Jeune

to André Breton's employer
          the couturier Doucet
     mentioned in Proust

then by the delicate
          maneuverings of art dealers
     Jacques Seligmann and Messmore

to Joan Whitney Payson
          a big strapping woman
     whose public passions

were horse racing and the Mets
          and who redecorated her
     Fifth Avenue apartment

in a *quite ghastly* shade
          derived from the reddish-brown
     patch of earth in the foreground   *Tomkins 57*

to her son John
          because of his deep feeling for it
     until March 30, 1987

the day van Gogh's *Sunflowers*
          was knocked down to the Yasudo
     Fire & Marine Insurance Company

for thirty-nine million
            nine hundred thousand dollars
        (*a whole new class of collectors*

Reagan-era tycoons
            who have made money very quickly
        in fields such as arbitrage

and corporate takeovers   *Tomkins 60*
            insider trading attractive
        to organized crime according to

the chief commonwealth fraud officer)   *Financial Post 3/30/88 3*
            because of rising insurance
        Irises spent the next year

in a Portland bank
            And then Sotheby's
        after having been saved

by Alfred Taubman a Detroit
            real-estate developer
        specializing in shopping centers

arranged the auction
            there had never been
        such a demand for tickets   *Tomkins 65*

(Gauguin: *A day will come*
            and I see it as if
        it had already come)   *Tomkins 45*

the bidding went slowly at first
            a moment of silence
        Vincent to Theo

It is enough to make you dizzy
            so why think about it?
        It would only daze our minds   *Tomkins 67*

and then Marion's gavel
        cracked down on the podium
    forty-nine million dollars

the room erupted
        in prolonged cheering
    the turntable revolved again

and the picture was gone   *Tomkins 66*

IV.xi

For Franz Schurmann and Sandy Close

Lolling on cushions
        at Esalen
    in the old Murphy residence

what a place to discuss
        aristocracy
    the hillside is dotted

outside the window
        with couples groping
    the lead person eyes closed

it is in this very room
        that Mike Murphy has explored
    with members of the KGB

how to add *cohesiveness*   *Tao Te Ching 60*
        to global life
    suddenly it becomes possible

to wander through vestiges
        the whole of mankind
    an imaginary museum

shall we visit the Angkor ruins
            take a stroll in the Tivoli?   *Ricoeur 278*
    and *expand frontiers*

that headiness first sensed
            at the United Nations
    the roof of the world

the open country
            of what transcends speech   *Sengchao; Wang Wei 120*
    Where now is Judith the black princess?

but as opposed to hereditary caste
            the so-called *élites*
    of our open society

competitive aggressive
            over-specialized workaholics
    all owing their status to the state

could only re-enact
            the rituals of sovereignty
    and not transcend them

and now Shevardnadze returning
            to raise Bay Area funds
    for his think tank in Moscow

while the two sea otters
            play to the slow rhythm
    of gleaming surf and kelp

my mother mistrusting
            Jung's theories of color
    for their symbolism

blue as serenity
            the Virgin's robe
    when *blue beside red*

is never blue beside blue
>> *Marc's Tower of Blue Horses*
> And what will prompt us if we see

that what we see is darkness?
> will we like Wordsworth
> look to the *unfathered*

vapour that lifts itself   *Prelude* 6.527
>> from the chasm within us?
> to the shepherd *stalking through the fog*?   *Prelude* 8.400-01

or to the people
> when they gather together
> as when on campus

with United People of Color
> we had Bishop Tutu
> descend from his helicopter

into the Greek Theater
> while the faculty monitors
> less than the fifty I had promised

were enough for the roughly peaceful
> parade to the Regents' meeting
> (provocateurs recognizable

and instantly neutralized
> by a crowd of friendly questions)   *Tao Te Ching* 60
> our music played

from the Chancellor's loudspeakers
> *tu n'es pas maître à ta maison*   *your house no longer yours*
> *quand nous y sommes*   *while we are there*

and only a little gratuitous
> tear gas from the Alameda Sheriffs
> Having taken

the issue of order on one street
        away from the police
    can we not envision

a peaceful million blocking
        Pennsylvania Avenue
    or Tienanmen Square

without unlocking the terror
        in the hearts of colonels
    that has always led to bloodbaths

and if this is craziness
        from which all the greatest
    benefits of Greece have sprung   *Nietzsche 21*

need it be tragic?
      Le monde   *The world*
      tend à la beauté   *tends toward beauty*   *Bachelard 38*

Under the stove
        through the half-opened door
    the shadow of the black cat's head

touches the shadow of the bowl
        Between the window
    and its dark half-opened frame

the slant L of moonlight

IV.xii

For Charles and Doris Muscatine

The Book of Opening the Mouth
    has been withdrawn
  meaning no one can find it

she hands me the hand-out
        about the devaluation of the dollar
    lack of funds for foreign publications

cutbacks in staffing
        if we are to maintain
    research-level collections

and so Wallis Budge
        who were yourself a librarian
    despite the assumptions

of first yours and now this empire
        about access without end
    you are thanks to Reagan's decade

of defense spending funded
        in the foreign money markets
    to remain lost

the darkness never banished very far
        threatens once more to return
    and though none of the fires

set in the 1970s
        burnt away these books
    those scooped-out drawers of cards

on perhaps St. Thomas Aquinas
        have never been replaced
    all three of my first books

on the once unspeakable subject
        of drugs and the CIA
    have been for what it is worth

missing since their purchase
        from the Main (not the Undergraduate) Library
    which is o.k. I wish myself

to forget everything about it
         except the importance of suppression
    which was enough in my case

to send me back again
         to hoarse Virgil and Tu Fu
    (does one have to assume

it was drug-crazed hippies
         burned out Wheeler Auditorium
    when the Administration had a project

to close down all large halls
         that could serve as meeting-places?)
    But then as a minor member

of the Golden Dawn
         on the staff of the British Museum
    with Binyon and Sir Aurel Stein

you believed anyway
         in shared secret truths
    as Rexroth shrewdly speculates

there was no way A.E. Waite
         was going to tell the whole story
    about the Rosicrucians   *Rexroth 244*

if every culture
         has grounded itself
    on some form of denial

perhaps all of us
         will have to read less and better
    above all more slowly

as when for three or four hundred years
         it was the one Book
    incessu humilis   lowly at first

successu excelsa   and then sublime   *Aug. Conf. 3.5; Auerbach '65 48*
          its psalms (accessible
       as Erasmus wrote

even to peasants in their fields)
             sung by choirs daily
          till their similes *the hart*

panteth after the water-brooks   *Psalm 42:1*
             reduced to archetypes
          that had the concentrated strength

not just to change Europe
             and abolish domestic slavery
          but to replace idols

with icons and then after
             so-called universal education
          symbolism images

those places of possibility
       within ourselves
    dark because they are hidden   *Lorde 282*

as the age of somnolence
             and odd eccentric genius
          yields to the hosts of the well-trained

and petty-minded
             lost and disempowered
          in the very equality

and diversity we praise

A lock of hair
        with its white streaks
    in the toilet bowl

the rest in the wastepaper basket
        so that is why during
    our last minutes together

before your three month practice
        period at Tassajara
    you wore a tuque to breakfast

Having imagined myself tonsured
        after one prayerful
    post-adolescent week

among the spring daffodils
        at La Pierre Qui Vire
    meeting you a sexy

History and Lit major at Radcliffe
        seemed like a providential
    escape from celibacy

you brought me back to earth
        I moved quickly to finish off
    that dissertation on Eliot

and mistook as the flattery
        of imitation
    your also writing on Eliot

the first hint that through years
        of growing towards each other
    we might intersect

and continue right on through
        as in time we came to watch
    the great elm behind

our zen-room window
        dropping and growing its leaves
    Then fighting too hard

as our children grew away
        in the latest decade
    of a thirty-year marriage

to show that in a world
        of apartness we two alone
    could go on sharing

led to 悶 *men*[4] (the heart gated)
        meaning *melancholy*
    or 愁 *ch'ou*[2] (the heart

in the autumn when rice fields burn)
        Did I drive you to priesthood?
    Did you drive me to the solitary

writing of this poem?
        Or was this shared drift
    towards separation

the clue to our happiness together?
        You have gone for three months
    to the canyon of Tassajara

so far off that at last
        you are again visible
    just as at last I see

becoming year by year
        busier
    than I ever thought I could manage

the ghost of our marriage
           like some great white bird
    we have lifted up

to fly off
           no longer counted on
    and thus liberated

what you practice now
           silence and chant in mountains
    pure sunlight

in the empty gate
           what I dreamt of then
    間 *chien*[1]

the space between
           among while
    a division of a house

to divide separate
           to blame
    to put a space between

to part friends

IV.xiv

For Fred and Betty Crews

What can one say when she
           whom we loved for her purity
    is put out for hire?

she will be brought down
           by the giants who embrace her
    but how to say this

in kindly fashion
          about those whom familiarity
          has conditioned me to think of as colleagues

having now just seen
          the debates of mystery
          and collegial discourse

dating back to the Middle Age
          whether *god has three selves*
          or *the author none*

the *neurotic Cartesian*
          quest for certainty   *Lang 128*
          used yet again to exclude

all those who might correct
          our reluctance to expand
          towards the boundaries of mind

Synge in his dream
          struggling *to remain quiet*
          holding my knees together

till every impulse of my body
          became a form of the dance   *Yeats '61 332*
          while admitting

those *literary Marxists*
          (a great sleep
          among the professors)   *Hill 57*

who write *for literary Marxists*
          solidarity yes
          but within a "field"   *Said '83A 149*

or contemplate the fruit
          of an open poetics
          from an *exploded self*   *Silliman; Nation 7/2–9/88*

without mystery
            a flourishing liberal community
    in which power is dispersed

and resistance hard to imagine   *Breslin 262*
            while on the other side
    these operational relationships

the CIA *considers*
            as perhaps its most sensitive   *Church Committee; Zinn 544*
    If Pound loving Mencius

(the humane man *has no enemy*)   *Mencius (tr. Legge)* 7B:3.3
            lost it fulminating
    against Socratic and Semitic

questioners and splitters   *Pound SP 85*
            how can I from some rostrum
    proclaim that truth has been lost

when so much money comes
            how they hold it and hug it
    and hunger after it

as dogs do for dry bones   *Hill 93*
            The Whore set up
    your colleges and schools   *Hill 156*

and yet how not from love
            be moved to criticize
    our English dear English

no longer the simple birthright
            of the English people
    the language from which I access

the great matrix of language
            parochializing Arnold's
    best that has been thought and said

Ransom's *Criticism Inc.*   P.D. Scott '91 17
          and those who now have the urge
       to embellish the Mona Lisa

with some variety of moustache
          giving up *the world entirely*
       for the aporias and unthinkable

paradoxes of a text   Said '83B 4
          and what use to say
       with Wordsworth *Go to the poets!*   Prelude 11.68

when by day we can no longer
          maintain the distance from the world
       it took to say *I am not*

and at night we no longer hear
          the muttering candle
       at the point of going out

the cat distending on the rug
          the drops on the roof
       the startling eucalyptus nut

and then the exhaust and return
          of simple breathing
       like the surf through the pines

outside the window
          all night at Big Sur
       and in their life they have never seen

beyond the torrent
          in the dew-wet meadow
       waist-high in flowers

the shadow of the eagle
          slant steeply up
       across the valley's headwall

over the ice fields
             snow and jagged cliff
       in the white sunlight

to where it lands   而不爭 *erh²* *pu⁴* *cheng¹*
                                               and does not strive Tao Te Ching 81

                    IV.xv

            For Maria

Not the self in the world
            so much as the world
      the self is in

but as I learned from marriage
            there are still areas
      where the past rises to haunt us

certain phrases from old pain
            which trigger the new
      now we too share these ghosts

as when you tell me once more
            I don't know if I can survive
      this feeling of abandonment

when you go off on your travels
            for which I can't blame you
      That's what she used to say

when the children were small
            I only want to hear
      that despite all I make you happy

our being together such a lift
            we can only profit But you do not speak
      except of being powerless So I say

                 164

Men make structures of their lives
          where they withdraw if feelings threaten
     and women? What is it that you do?

The more I know the more women are
          a complete mystery You say *We rant and rail*
     That's all we can do And we go back to sleep

This morning at breakfast
          I brew Darjeeling and read the *Times*
     how *Mrs. Huffington*

says Picasso beat Dora Maar
          into unconsciousness and *ground*
     his lighted cigarette into Françoise's cheek

leaving a scar that still remains
          When two of his lovers
     demanded he choose between them

he told them to fight it out themselves
          He continued to paint as they wrestled
     later describing the scene

as "one of my choicest memories"
          One *suffered a breakdown*
     one *hanged herself*

one *shot herself in the head*
          he *rejected all of his children*   *New York Times 6/3/88*
     his grandson poisoned himself

Is this the tension
          between great art and happiness
     why Rilke *discovered*

his unsuitability for domestic life?   *Rilke '82 xxvii*
          I had always assumed (not knowing)
     that to kiss and fondle too many breasts

would leave in the end a bitterness
      like this teapot's second brew
   that one would come to experience

sex as quotation parody
     women's faces and bodies
    tortured disassembled   New York Times 6/3/88

by logical energies   Yeats '61 289
     a problem with modernity
   too much faith in experience

art requires ruthlessness
     Aren't you better off
   with me than Picasso? Yet even Maylie

tears in her eyes said *Remember*
     Maria is powerless Somehow we women
   must do things differently We are drawn

to the wrong men But I remember
     going to Sausalito We strolled hand in hand
   through the stalled tourist traffic

you smiled (*Look!*) at every cat
     all the world knew we were happy lovers
   that's what I'm grateful for

What is wrong about that?

IV.xvi

For Daniel and Patricia Ellsberg

The colors of dawn
     creep east from the blazing windows
   of San Francisco across the bay

the perspective from this hilltop
    and from morning za-zen
   a sense of well-being

well-being not *non-being*   *Tworkov 250*
    shrinking yesterday's pleasure
   in the successful compromise resolution

that merely smoothed over differences
    the spirit of chancery
   learnt in Ottawa so long ago

now powerless as we wait
    for a war in the Middle East
   that will be too big for resolutions

and direct action
    from conviction of one's rightness
   now part of the general cacophony

at what point
    do the smoothing over of differences
   and the conviction of rightness

themselves engender nightmare
    we are so good at forgetting
   photos from Ustaša prisoners   *Croatian terrorist*

(risky to cite this
    hate-ridden book
   that arrived in my mail

but how to ignore it
    when so many of its claims
   are indeed corroborated?)

showing one man with a victim's head
    another with a heart held high   *Manhattan 77, 109*
   a neck being severed

with a Swedish saw
        a necklace of cut out eyes
        another of tongues   *Manhattan 78*

while the eyes of the torturers
        so far as one can see them
        in the dark recesses of the photos

are slitted like masks
        their stare not so much passionate as crazed
        and strangely calm

transported beyond the unnerving
        fabric of compassion
        (where evil is constrained

to the limits of ignorance
        by memory of inner warmth)
        with the knowledge they are inspired

(as in today's throat-cuttings
        for the hero of the Ramayana)   *PBS 11/1/90*
        by a conception of love

some of the worst atrocities
        by *members of the Franciscan order*
        one danced at a massacre

a macabre dance in his soutane   *Singleton 197*
        the Poglavnik Pavelić
        cordially received by the Pope   *Singleton 88*

compared by one bishop to Christ   *Singleton 197*
        unworthy of Christ's disciples
        to think that the struggle against evil

could be waged in a noble way   *Singleton 197*
        (the smiles all calmly
        directed towards the camera

as at a chapel consecration)
   Cardinal Tisserant
  the only important Catholic voice

to speak out against the slaughter   *Lernoux 287*
   (dilemmas of church and power
  even more visible

now that Serbs are the aggressors)
   while *even the Germans and Italians*
  intervened on occasions

to restrain the Ustaša
   from their more extreme brutalities   *Singleton 89*
  might not this massacre

of *some 350,000*   *Singleton 88*
   or is it *a million*   *Anderson 38*
  have been averted in '34

if Laval and Eden
   to keep Italy in the league
  had not blocked the extradition

of the assassins of the king
   with a *compromise resolution*
  that *denounced terrorism*   *Hoptner 27-28*

but failed to censure Italy
   for Ciano's funds to Pavelić *Vucinich 43; Manhattan 12-14*
  the same Pavelić

whom Ciano continued to meet
   (with *his band of cut-throats*)   *Ciano 202, 333-34; cf. 61*
  an aggressive calm man

who knows where he wants to go
   and does not fear to take responsibility   *Ciano 202*
  (*necessary however*

to prepare the ground
        with London and Paris)   *Ciano 201*
    in the spirit of chancery

and whom after World War II
        now a major war criminal
    the U.S. and Vatican

helped exfiltrate to Argentina
        after Dulles' secret negotiations
    with Rauff the designer

of the mobile gas oven   *P.D. Scott '86B 12*
        via the Rat Line
        Ustascha membership compulsory   *U.S. State Dept. Report 7/16/46;*
                                                    Anderson 39, 295
funded with SS gold   *P.D. Scott '86B 11*
        (Hoettl and Schwend
        now working for the Americans)   *P.D. Scott '86B 14;*
                                                    Linklater 135, 162, 296
and Pavelić's own plunder
        cached in the salt caverns
    of the Salzkammergut   *Hoettl 321-26*

for a new era
        mercenaries in the Congo
    a few hijackings in the 1970's

some ambassadors assassinated   *Anderson 41*
        Durcansky and Baresić
    in the World Anti–Communist League   *Hoettl 323; Anderson 41*

but the big money for Gehlen
        (Judge Peck the *Kameradenwerk*)   *postwar SS net*
    the Paradise Island Bridge Company   *Mahon 33-58;*
                                            Seldes 120, 302-05, 328
the cocaine coup in Bolivia   *Marshall 68-71*
        insertion of red-hot wires
    into the ears of the victims

in *the practical demonstration*
        of *interrogation techniques*   *Linklater 301*
    no! not original sin

(a hardened member of the military
       sick with horror
    as they *died in agony)*   *Linklater 301*

but civilization
      become an idol
    vacant glass eyes blazing

and its sins to come
      the torturer *stripped to the waist*
    and with his torso oiled   *Linklater 298*

shot while extradited   *Linklater 306*
      delle Chiaie his mentor
    in the Bologna railway station bombing

the strategy of tension
      as with DINA and the Argentinians   *Linklater 278;*
    helped in his escape   *Marshall, 70*

by what we call *intelligence*   *Linklater 300*
      the spirit of chancery
    blind to the autumn sunlight

kindling the leaves above us

IV.xvii

For Andrew Reding, John Stockwell, and Bill Johnson

Tonight by the L-shaped swimming pool
      we two resume this morning's conversation
    when we watched the two bald eagles

glide up to the distant nest
   built by the rangers
  (we learnt from talking to them)

from steel re-bars after
   the first nest in the cottonwood
  fell into the artificial lake

an odd place Andrew to be talking
   of Tomás Borge
  though he too spoke of *The Lake*

As Mirror Of Our Values   *Reding 85*
   and opposed to *the theology of death*   *Reding 119*
  the geography of love

a matter of foresight
   to forestall vengeance   *Reding 121*
  as when Borge himself

confronted the Somocista
   who had raped and murdered his wife
  and said *My revenge*

will be to pardon you   *Reding 1, 46*
   beside that river
  where the woman has been hiding

for a long time
   I was frightened my baby
  would begin to cry

and they would kill him   *Alegría*
   Not the newspapers' Borge
  Czech advisers for the police

the false bourgeois principle
   that all men are equal
  the working class's

fundamental obligation
            is the consolidation of their power   *Leiken 230-31*
      you give me instead

Borge quoting from St. Francis
            I do not wish to belong to any order
            I have had a divine revelation

that I am a new fool   *Reding 113*
            or from St. Hilary *the rich*
      are either thieves

or sons of thieves   *Reding 121*
            I think of St. Augustine
      we were astonished to hear

of works in the true faith
            almost in our own times   *Conf. 8.6.6*
      when I consider the passion

reminding me of myself
            in my early twenties
      which took you to Central America

to interview Mora and Figueres
            and brings you now
      to this Conference on World Affairs

John Stockwell has denounced
            as organized at least in part
      by his former boss in the CIA   *Stockwell 102*

Bill Johnson who before that
            was a poet and editor
      with Angleton of *Furioso*

as I learnt on a panel
            with his close friend Howard Nemerov
      and so late at night having walked

away with my half-finished plate
    of cold Alaska salmon
  from my half-serious proposal

to guarantee free speech at Berkeley
    for the FBI legal adviser
  the more serious disagreement

with the Moscow Institute expert
    over Lithuania
  half angry at myself

to be so easily flattered
    (we must be always of two minds
  about this civilization

that joins politeness
    and enlargement of discourse
  to the enlargement of violence

for whatever it takes
    to maintain inequality)
  I come at last in the narrow corridor

to the music room Bill Johnson
    drinking Moosehead like myself
  and we talk about the fifties

those little magazines
    their ironic notes on culture
  and the talk goes so easily

(will John forgive me for this?)   *John Stockwell*
    I wonder why I cannot
  ask him about Borge

hidden by Ernesto Cardenal
    at the Solentiname
  community of fishermen

his old message *Strife breaks out*
       because righteousness
       is nowhere to be found   *Habakkuk* 1:3-4; *Reding 123*

or his new *You cannot serve*
       both God and riches   *Reding 118*
       Christ isn't going to come

because Christ is here
       and is never going to leave   *Reding 83*
       (the woman has been hiding a long time)

my half-angry other self
       watching as if through the window
       wonders if this half-ability to chat

across old battlelines
       can signify more than
       the failure of old dreams

of that magnetic sureness
       that impelled you Andrew Reding
       to spend years in Central America

myself just ten years ago
       stricken with hepatitis
       to accept this selfish

liberating decision
       Generosity would make me a book   *Sartre 121; Hyde 40*
       the spirit everywhere

I had the actual sense
       of a Presence
       I wept for joy   *Roethke 23-24; Hyde 145*

and in history itself
       language tending toward
       its *root nature of freedom*

that *has nothing to do with bondage*
        against the doubleness
    that history does not change

Gemeinschaft Gesellschaft
        peace from dominion
    peace from justice

and in the third millennium
peace from love

IV.xviii

For Carolyn Merchant and Charles Sellers

This morning silence
        no song birds my eyes open
    there deep in the shadows

of our small back-yard privet
        an out-sized hawk
    as once above my grandfather's

lake near Ste. Agathe
        of the two I am
    the more carefully watched

by an eye full of darkness
        like Breton at Ste. Agathe
    la profondeur de l'étang   *the depth of the pond*

dans l'oeil de l'oiseau   *in the eye of the bird*
        imagining himself escaped   Breton 140-41
    from *the insanity of the hour*   Balakian 205

la rame immobile de l'épervier   *the hawk's unmoving wing*
        dans son coeur s'allume une lampe   *in its heart a lamp is lit*
    qui permet de voir   *making it possible to see*

tout ce qui se passe en lui   *what is going on inside him*
          at no loss to renew myths   Breton 140
      L'ésotérisme   *The esoterism*

de champ illimité   *of unlimited scope*
          dont dispose l'homme   *which is available to us*
      in that time of war   Breton 152

La vieille Egypte
          n'a su mieux figurer   *could not have figured better*
      les circonstances   *the circumstances*

qui entourent   *surrounding*
          la conception d'un dieu   *the conception of a god*
      from the Laurentian silence   Breton 142

his well-trained European mind
          hearing easily
      what we could so easily believe: *Osiris*

est un dieu noir   *is a black god*   Breton 154
          (a great hawk
      seated in a boat

which hath the white crown on his head   Budge 329
          Give me my mouth
      that I may speak with it

May I follow my heart
          at its season of fire and night)   Budge 26
      versus Aragon *il est temps*   *it is time*

d'en finir avec   *to finish with*
          les hallucinations   *all hallucinations*   Browder 127
      Artaud by then

in a mental asylum
          Crevel a suicide   Camus 93
      Pound only saved by the fluke

he could not have depended on
            of his incarceration
        to hear silence

to see the hawk in the dawn
            briefly gain and then lose
        its shadow

that lake smaller and duller
            in that *contrée énorme*   *enormous country*
        où tout se tait   *where all is silent*   Breton 60

than I remember it
            once the mirror
        I could not free of dust

now itself dust
            a cracked photograph
        the silence I imagined

the absence of those expelled
            as from the wood in Oka
        where on a cold November night

I once watched the coal-sack nebula
            a wood whose sanctity
        a child could feel

now filled with cries and gunshots
            sucked into the uproar
        of the United Nations

while the gorged waterfalls
            of Yosemite Canyon
        I first saw in a magenta

three-cent U.S. postage stamp
            at the time of Breton's manifesto
        have since drenched me

and swept me downwards in time
        free from imagined roots
    the torrent of words

making history first a road
        then a painted curtain
    or memory first a comfort

opening the mind
        and then an idol
    our life a paradox

that cannot be allowed
        to subside into a mere
    affirmation

or the voice surprised
        by a visitation
    to lapse into authority

these moments for which
        we can only be grateful
    in need of no other praise

so what am I doing
        who have lost the dream
    of controlling darkness

the black intelligence
        the divination
    of the mysteries of the night   *Balakian 207*

what does the simplicity
        of this hawk's gaze mean
    in my back yard

besides that the birdsong stops?

V

V.i

For Brian Willson

A man before a train
        and the train does not stop
    its crew put in fear

of a sitting Gandhian
        on whom the FBI has opened
    a file as a *terrorist*   *Stockwell 105-06*

you are dragged over ties and gravel
        skull sprung open both legs lost
    and history changed

by thus concentrating
        mind and body together
    on a pure point of conviction

the pure principles of Jefferson
        our leaders seem never to have heard of
    and for which you are still ready to die

we can lever the world   *move without moving; Tao Te Ching 69*
        these words are *very simple*
    no one can practice them   *Tao Te Ching 70*

does this make you a man of the future
        or are you one of the last
    to inhabit the Fourth of July

while others into whose mind
        the dream of the city has fled
    no longer citizens at all

when what we mean by a civilized person
        one whose systems of denial
    are so perfect such breaches of decorum

are no longer to be expected
        and why would a civilized person
    choose your life so lonely

even your wife cannot stand it?
        those watching the ebb of power
    mostly taking refuge

in Rilke's temple of elsewhere
        there was a bird on the lake
    spoke to us in childhood

out of what we were not
        more clearly than any book
    but those whom commitment

has driven into isolation
        can meet at that cone's point
    the place not where we began

but where we converge
        as when you Dan in Moscow   *Daniel Ellsberg*
    met and talked with Sakharov

until four in the morning
        I believe in the *paradiso interno*
    the wheat gold light   *Rumi '84 46* (1937)

not ever present
           but the spring of discourse
     when the heart is at ease   *Omar* 118

becoming more and more audible
           from the growing concert
     The way

cannot enlarge the person
           a person can enlarge the way   *Confucius Analects* 15.28;
     of its witnesses   *Bodhidharma 73*

in humane disagreement
           (the Gospel of Thomas
     when you make the inner as the outer

then shall ye enter)   *Logia 22*
           as to what most matters
     how *to seek for the lost mind*   *Mencius* 6A:11.4

so while others praise you
           for making the train stop
     using non-involvement to steer the world   *Tao Te Ching* 57

I am drawn towards
           your simplicity
     this world you are *in* not *of*

held in focus not just
           by saying *No!* to the state   *Mencius* 7B:11
     (when intelligence and cleverness arise

so does hypocrisy
           when a nation falls into darkness
     we have patriotic ministers)   *Tao Te Ching* 18

but by without eagerness
           being ready to die
     for what you truly believe

this is truly believing
               hard for those whose experience
         of death has generally been removed

to other peoples far off
               so we believe almost nothing
         it would be folly

to try to explain this
               to the well-educated
         who would rather read de Sade

than what we do to our victims
               like those who believed
         that the freight cars

were taking them
to a better life

                    V.ii

         For Alan Williamson

My life an act of faith
               in the future?
         but the future is not our future

a fellowship of learning
               without competitiveness
         an end to mere acquisition

of wealth or of women
               hegemonic cynicisms
         from a lack of faith

no! after a lifetime
               trying to save America
         from a rendezvous with karma

and its tragic deconstructions
        from the Sicilian Expedition
    to the Suez Crisis

I have to acknowledge
        I never let go enough
    to be healed by the night's breath
                              夜氣 *yeh⁴ ch'i⁴*
                                 Mencius 6A:8.2

and if those sixties communes
        where one debated
    the privacy of toothbrushes or bodies

were late cultural artifacts
        what else shall we say
    of the sanghas of the nineties

as Maureen Stuart said
        they attract very immature people
    and breed *a kind of solipsism*

a very limited interpretation
                                  Tworkov 165-66
        perhaps in memory
    of Baker Roshi lecturing

on the *mischievousness without form*
        in even a Bodhisattva's heart
    shortly before

the Zen Center Board Meeting
        which led to his departure
    Lou Hartman the senior monk

once assigned to clean up
        the liquor bottles after
    one of the governor's private parties

a kind of elitist Skull and Bones society
                                   Tworkov 235
        women angry about sex
    men angry about money
                                 Tworkov 241-42

but as one woman asked
        How could we bitch about
  the white BMW

when he was driving to the airport
        with Mike Murphy of Esalen
  to work with the Russians

against a nuclear holocaust?   *Tworkov 237*
        while back in Montreal
  Judy's eyes filled with tears

in the midst of the panic
        that her regent Osël Tenzin
  might have given the community AIDS

as she affirmed his shortcomings
        were a test of her practice
  Was the Zen Center Mess

(celebrated by feminists and anarchists
        for *stopping the teacher*)   *Tworkov 243*
  a cooptation *by the bureaucratic*

machinations of the democratic process
        or an end to *obsolete autocracy*?   *Tworkov 203*
  and will the future

belong to the *very immature*
        or to those few whose practice
  sinking to the most forgotten

returning to the origin
        and bringing something back   *Eliot '33 119*
  recovers a Great Memory

in the midst of a Great Regression
        such as at times before
  has afflicted the world

and returned it to focus
       to preserve those gradations
    (*mind* in Confucius

Mencius: *to seek root mind*   *Mencius 6A:10.8, 11.4*
       root mind which is *root Buddha)*   *Bodhidharma 8*
    language that let Wang Wei

having bowed to the emperor
    compared to whose brilliance
    the sun's is dimmer   *Wang Wei 98*

see *solitude a joy*   *Wang Wei 141*
       and *listen with empty spirit*   *Chuang Tzu 57-58; Wang Wei 5*
    the dharma itself *a raft*

which is abandoned   *Lu K'uan Yu, 133*
    the antelope in mid-hop
    hung by a single prong

not treading on the path of reason
    or falling into the net of words   *Yan Yu 24; Wang Wei 15*
    and then empowered Tu Fu

having wasted his life
    on pavilion portraits   *Tu Fu 96*
    remembering his wife's *jade arms*   *Tu Fu 25*

to control new fields
    of *syntactic ambiguity*   *Tu Fu ix*
    at the sight of the K'uei-chou women

hair turned half-white
    still waiting for husbands
    in this relentless ruin of war   *Tu Fu 76*

and gives those whose limit
    from the luck
    of having experienced

a youthful derangement from the world
        is a sense of well-being
     not of non–being   *Tworkov 250*

who now sit eyes half-closed
        facing the window
     not the wall behind

thus in their way at home
        with the great family
     by seeking not following

the enduring practice
        to remain still
     as this tiny spider

sails in the breath eddies
        beneath the nose cliff
     until at last it can fix

its minute thread
below the eye

V.iii

For all friends

As if all I needed was somehow
        to imagine together
     as if at a party

those who made me so grateful
        I had no wish but *to pass it on*
     that early need to define self

in terms of existential ironies
        what we are and are not
     lost in a different focus

so clear blue sky is blue
   and voices so long inaudible
  either silent altogether

or at my side like Ronna saying
   Just because you're a poet
  you don't have to be miserable

a party to make everyone happy
   at least while it happens
  like my parents' parties at Christmas

writers painters amateur politicians
   amused by each others' differences
  Jean Palardi's *chansons de bois*

behavior so gratuitous
   including wild argument
  staircase dancing

an adult peeing on the kitchen floor
   the future
  entered into us

and was changed by us   Rilke
   or last July's hot summer night
  walking up De Bullion Street

to the Place St. Louis
   the grandmother on her shooting stick
  nodding to the triadic beat

of the Greek harpist
   beside a stack of his cassettes
  then slowly moving to the asphalt

pathway and starting to waltz
   by herself first and then
  with a younger woman

whose style was smart and ballroom
   while hers I imagined was that
  of a village on the lower St. Lawrence

you could see not by driving to it
   but in the distance of her eyes
  How many years since we were free

to walk this way in a U.S.
   city at midnight? even in Berkeley
  city of metamorphosis in a dream

of magic transformation
   from pupas into butterflies
  all night the impoverished

desperately searching the war zone
   of the inner city for cocaine
  while we are still mostly after dark

imprisoned in hillside houses
   our views of moonlit Alcatraz
  a stupor a narcosis you have to leave

the country to be aware of
   to be of that mind
  we see we are already

where we are trying to get to
   a truth so simple
  it takes a lifetime

to reach this awareness
   the other shore is this one   *Bodhidharma 51*
  this is her youthful dance

the *unsayable* like Hegel's rose   *Rilke '82 201; Hegel 11*
   not in some *other realm*   *Rilke '82 199*
  forest parks or lakeside pavilions   *Bodhidharma 31*

but the joy
           always available to us
       of this spine-hung breathing

that holds the earth
           close up against the strained
       cross of legs beneath

and no longer is
           but watches the poisoned mind
       and this second joy

we only stumble upon
           somehow to have this party
       It is not good to be alone   *Gen.* 2:18

there is still this need to praise
           how happy a thing can be   *Rilke '82 201*
       and like that Dorset potter

whose wheel this child once turned
           to share silently
       in augmenting the ceaseless

creation of the world
           even the sutras say
       Go beyond language   *Bodhidharma 44*

and if the excitement of childhood
           is now elusive
       at least to put irony behind us

and so deeply inhabit
           the night's silences
       that the owl on Grizzly Peak

becomes effortlessly (surprise!)
           the whip-poor-will
       heard when the candle

SOURCES

Alegría, Claribel. *Woman of the River*. Pittsburgh: University of Pittsburgh Press, 1989.

Anderson, Scott, and Jon Lee Anderson. *Inside the League*. New York: Dodd Mead, 1986.

Auerbach, Erich. *Literary Language and Its Public in Late Latin Antiquity and in the Middle Ages*. New York: Pantheon Books, 1965.

Auerbach, Erich. "Philology and Weltliteratur." Translated by M. and E.W. Said. *Centennial Review,* 1969.

Bachelard, Gaston. *L'Eau et les Reves*. Paris: José Corti, 1942.

Balakian, Anna. *André Breton: Magus of Surrealism*. New York: Oxford University Press, 1971.

Bennett, Donna. "On the Margin: Looking for a Literary Identity." *Candian Forum,* April 1987.

Bernstein, Charles, with Bruce Andrews. *The* L=A=N=G=U=A=G=E *Book*. Carbondale, IL: Southern Illinois University Press, 1984.

Bodhidharma. *The Zen Teaching of Bodhidharma*. Translated by Red Pine. San Francisco: North Point Press, 1989.

Borduas, Paul Emile. *Ecrits/Writings 1942–1958*. Halifax: Press of the Nova Scotia College of Art, 1978.

Breslin, James E.B. *From Modern to Contemporary: American Poetry, 1945–1965*. Chicago: University of Chicago Press, 1984.

Breton, André. *Arcane 17*. New York: Brentano's, 1945.

Browder, Clifford. *André Breton*. Geneva: Droz, 1967.

Budge, E.A. Wallis. *The Book of the Dead: The Papyrus of Ani in the British Museum*. New York: Dover, 1967.

CIV/n: A Literary Magazine of the 50's, edited by Aileen Collins. Montreal: Véhicule Press, 1983.

Camus, Albert. *The Rebel: An Essay on Man in Revolt*. New York: Vintage, 1956.

Carew Manuscripts Preserved in the Archi-episcopal Library at Lambeth. London: Longman's Green, 1868.

Carpenter, Edmund. *Eskimo Realities*. New York: Holt, Rinehart and Winston, 1973.

Chomsky, Noam. *Turning the Tide: U.S. Intervention in Central America and the Struggle for Peace*. Boston: South End Press, 1985.

Chomsky, Noam. *see also* Herman, Edward S. and Noam Chomsky.

Chuang Tzu. *The Complete Works of Chuang Tzu*. Translated by Burton Watson. New York: Columbia University Press, 1970.

Church Committee: U.S. Congress. Senate Select Committee to Study Government Operations with Respect to Intelligence Activities, Vol. 1. Washington: Government Printing Office, 1976.

Ciano, Galeazzo. *Ciano's Diary 1939–1943*. London: Heinemann, 1947.

Clampitt, Amy. *The Kingfisher*. New York: Knopf, 1983.

Collard, Edgar Andrew. *Montreal: The Days That Are No More*. New York and Toronto: Doubleday, 1976.

Collins, Anne. *In the Sleep Room*. Toronto: Lester and Orpen Dennys, 1988.

Creeley, Robert. *For Love: Poems 1950–1960*. New York: Charles Scribner's Sons, 1962.

Creeley, Robert. "Introduction to *The New Writing in the USA*," (1965). In *The Poetics of the New American Poetry*, edited by Donald Allen and Warren Tallman. New York: Grove Press, 1973.

Cummings, Bruce. *The Origins of the Korean War. Volume II: The Roaring of the Cataract 1947–1950*. Princeton: Princeton University Press, 1990.

De Rachewiltz, Mary. *Discretions: Ezra Pound, Father and Teacher*. New York: New Directions, 1975.

Djwa, Sandra. *The Politics of the Imagination: A Life of F.R. Scott*. Toronto: McClelland & Stewart, 1987.

Doan Van Toai. "Vietnam: How We Deceived Ourselves." *Commentary*, March 1986.

Du, Nguyen. *The Tale of Kieu*. Translated by Huynh Sanh Thong. New Haven: Yale University Press, 1983.

Du Bois, Cora. "The 1870 Ghost Dance." In Heizer, R.F., and

M.A. Whipple (eds.), *The California Indians: A Source Book*.
    Berkeley and Los Angeles: University of California Press,
    1971.

Dudek, Louis. *Dk/ Some Letters of Ezra Pound*. Montreal: DC
    Books, 1974.

Duncan, Robert. "From a Notebook," (1954). In *The Poetics of the
    New American Poetry*, edited by Donald Allen and Warren
    Tallman. New York: Grove Press, 1973.

Duncan, Robert. "Towards an Open Universe," (1966). In *The
    Poetics of the New American Poetry*, edited by Donald Allen
    and Warren Tallman. New York: Grove Press, 1973.

Earl, Gordon. *A History of the Church and Parish of St. Michael and
    All Angels Croston*. Preston, Lancs.: Oliver Amey Ltd.,
    Printers, n.d.

Eberhart, Richard. *Of Poetry and Poets*. Urbana, Ill.: University of
    Illinois Press, 1977.

Eliot, T.S., *Selected Essays*. London: Faber and Faber, 1932.

Eliot, T.S., *The Use of Poetry and the Use of Criticism*. London:
    Faber, 1933.

Fekete, John. "Descent into the New Maelstrom: Introduction." In
    *The Structural Allegory: Reconstructive Encounters With the
    New French Thought*, edited by John Fekete. Minneapolis:
    University of Minnesota Press, 1984.

Fiedler, Leslie A. "A Postscript to the Rosenberg Case." *Encounter*,
    October 1953.

Font, Fray Pedro. *Font's Complete Diary: A Chronicle of the Founding
    of San Francisco*. Edited by Herbert Eugene Bolton.
    Berkeley: University of California Press, 1931.

Foster, Hal, ed. *The Anti-Aesthetic*. Port Townsend, Washington:
    Bay Press, 1983.

FRUS: U.S. Department of State. *Foreign Relations of the United
    States*. Washington: Government Printing Office, 1948.

Frye, Northrop. *Anatomy of Criticism: Four Essays*. Princeton:
    Princeton University Press, 1957.

Frye, Northrop. "Conclusion." In *Literary History of Canada:
    Canadian Literature in English*, edited by Carl F. Klinck.
    Toronto: University of Toronto Press, 1967.

Geertz, Clifford. *The Interpretation of Cultures*. New York: Basic
    Books, 1973.

Gimbutas, Marija. "The Beginning of the Bronze Age in Europe and the Indo-Europeans: 3500-2500 B.C." *Journal of Indo-European Studies*, 1973.

Ginsberg, Allen. *Allen Verbatim: Lectures on Poetry, Politics, Consciousness.* New York: McGraw-Hill, 1974.

Graff, W.L. *Rainer Maria Rilke: Creative Anguish of a Modern Poet.* New York: Greenwood Press, 1969.

Greenblatt, Stephen. *Renaissance Self-Fashioning: From More to Shakespeare.* Chicago and London: University of Chicago Press, 1980.

Greenblatt, Stephen. *Shakespearean Negotiations: The Circulation of Social Energy in Renaissance England.* Berkeley and Los Angeles: University of California Press, 1988.

Greenblatt, Stephen. "Towards a Poetics of Culture." In *The New Historicism*, edited by H. Aram Veeser. New York and London: Routledge, 1989.

Habermas, Jurgen. "Modernity—an Incomplete Project." In *The Anti-Aesthetic*, edited by Hal Foster. Port Townsend, Washington: Bay Press, 1983.

Hass, Robert. *Twentieth Century Pleasures: Prose on Poetry.* New York: Ecco Press, 1984.

Hegel, Georg Wilhelm Friedrich. *Philosophy of Right.* Oxford: Clarendon Press, 1942.

Heizer, Robert F. *The Destruction of California Indians.* Santa Barbara: Peregrine Smith, 1974.

Heizer, Robert F. *Federal Concern About Conditions of California Indians, 1853 to 1913.* Eight documents. Socorro, New Mexico: Ballena Press, 1979.

Herbert, Zbigniew. *Selected Poems.* Translated by Czeslaw Milosz and Peter Dale Scott. Harmondsworth, Middlesex: Penguin, 1968.

Herbert, Zbigniew, with Jaćek Trznadel. "An Interview With Zbigniew Herbert." *Partisan Review*, 1987.

Herman, Edward S. and Noam Chomsky. *Manufacturing Consent: The Political Economy of the Mass Media.* New York: Pantheon Books, 1988.

Heron, Woodburn (Introduction by D.O. Hebb). "Cognitive and Physiological Effects of Perceptual Isolation." In *Sensory Deprivation: A Symposium Held at Harvard Medical School,*

edited by Philip Solomon *et al.* Cambridge, MA: Harvard
University Press, 1961.

Hill, Christopher. *The Experience of Defeat: Milton and Some
Contemporaries.* New York: Viking, 1984.

Hinckle, Warren, and William Turner. *The Fish Is Red: The Story of
the Secret War Against Castro.* New York: Harper and Row,
1981.

Hoettl, William. *Hitler's Paper Weapon.* London: Rupert Hart-Davis,
1955.

Hoptner, J.B. *Yugoslavia in Crisis, 1934–1941.* New York:
Columbia University Press, 1962.

Howe, Fanny. "Silliman's 'Paradise'." *Poetics Journal Number 6,*
1986.

Hyde, Lewis. *The Gift: Imagination and the Erotic Life of Property.*
New York: Vintage Books, 1983.

Jaynes, Julian. *The Origin of Consciousness in the Breakdown of the
Bicameral Mind.* Boston: Houghton Mifflin, 1982.

K'ang Hsi. *The Sacred Edict.* Edited by F.W. Baller. Shanghai:
American Presbyterian Mission Press, 1892.

Kavanagh, Patrick J. *The Perfect Stranger.* London: Chatto and
Windus, 1966.

Kinnell, Galway. "Poetry, Personality, and Death." In *Claims for
Poetry,* edited by Donald Hall. Ann Arbor: University of
Michigan Press, 1982.

Kippenberg, Katherine. *Rainer Maria Rilke, Ein Beitrag.* Leipzig:
Insel-Verlag, 1935.

Kuberski, Philip. "Ego, Scriptor: Pound's Odyssean Writing."
Paideuma, Spring 1985.

Lang, Berel. "Rorty Scrivener." *Salmagundi,* Fall 1990–Winter
1991.

Lee, Martin A., and Bruce Shlain. *Acid Dreams: The CIA, LSD,
and the Sixties Rebellion.* New York: Grove Press, 1985.

Lehmann, Rosamond. *The Swan in the Evening.* London: Collins,
1967.

Leiken, Robert, and Barry Rubin. *The Central America Crisis Reader.*
New York: Summit Books, 1987.

Lernoux, Penny. *People of God: The Struggle for World Catholicism.*
New York: Viking, 1989.

Lescarbot, Marc. *Voyages of Jacques Cartier.* In *The History of New*

France, vol. II. Translated by W.L. Grant. Toronto: Champlain Society, 1911.

Levertov, Denise. *The Poet in the World*. New York: New Directions, 1973.

Linklater, Magnus, Isabel Hilton, and Neal Ascherson. *The Nazi Legacy: Klaus Barbie and the International Fascist Connection* New York: Holt, Rinehart and Winston, 1984.

Lorde, Audre. "Poems Are Not Luxuries." In *Claims for Poetry*, edited by Donald Hall. Ann Arbor: University of Michigan Press, 1982.

Lu K'uan Yu. *Ch'an and Zen Teaching: Series Two*. Edited by Charles Luk. Berkeley: Shambala, 1971.

Lyotard, François. *La Condition postmoderne*. Paris: Minuit, 1979.

Mahon, Gigi. *The Company that Bought the Boardwalk: A Reporter's Story of How Resorts International Came to Atlantic City*. New York: Random House, 1980.

Makin, Peter. *Provence and Pound*. Berkeley and Los Angeles: University of California Press, 1978.

Manhattan, Avro. *The Vatican's Holocaust*. Springfield, MO: Ozark Books, 1986.

Marcuse, Herbert. *Eros and Civilization: A Philosophical Inquiry into Freud*. Boston: Beacon Press, 1955.

Marks, John. *The Search for the "Manchurian Candidate."* New York: Times Books, 1979.

Massie, Suzanne. *Land of the Firebird: The Beauty of Old Russia*. New York: Simon and Schuster, 1980.

Merton, Thomas. *Confessions of a Guilty Bystander*. New York: Doubleday/Image, 1968.

Milosz, Czeslaw. *The Separate Notebooks*. New York: Ecco Press, 1984.

Milosz, Czeslaw. "Interview." *New York Review of Books*, February 27, 1986.

Montaigne, Michael Lord of. *Essayes*. Translated by Florio. London: Dent, 1929.

Montaigne, Michel de. *Essais*. Paris: Garnier, n.d.

Montrose, Louis A. "Professing the Renaissance: The Poetics and Politics of Culture." In *The New Historicism*, edited by H. Aram Veeser. New York and London: Routledge, 1989.

Naipaul, V.S. "Our Universal Civilization." *New York Review of*

Books, January 31, 1991.

Nietzsche, Friedrich. *The Anti-Christ*. Harmondsworth, Middlesex: Penguin, 1968.

Olson, Charles. "Projective Verse." In *The Poetics of the New American Poetry*, edited by Donald Allen and Warren Tallman. New York: Grove Press, 1973.

Pearson, Drew. *Diaries 1949–1959*. New York: Holt, Rinehart and Winston, 1974.

Pecora, Vincent P. "The Limits of Local Knowledge." In *The New Historicism*, edited by H. Aram Veeser. New York and London: Routledge, 1989.

Perelman, Bob. "Good and Bad/Good and Evil: Pound, Celine, and Fascism." *Poetics Journal Number 6*, 1986.

Pilat, Oliver. *Drew Pearson: An Unauthorized Biography*. New York: Pocket Books, 1973.

Plath, Sylvia. *The Bell Jar*. New York: Bantam, 1972.

Plath, Sylvia. *The Journals of Sylvia Plath*. New York: Ballantine, 1983.

Popper, Karl. *The Open Society and Its Enemies*. Princeton: Princeton University Press, 1950.

Pound, Ezra. *Cantos*. New York: New Directions, 1972.

Pound, Ezra. *Selected Prose 1909–1965*. New York: New Directions, 1973.

Read, Sir Herbert. "Recent Tendencies in Abstract Painting." *Canadian Art*, 1958.

Reaney, James. *A Suit of Nettles*. Toronto: Macmillan Company of Canada, 1958.

Reding, Andrew. *Christianity and Revolution: Tomás Borge's Theology of Life*. Maryknoll, N.Y.: Orbis Books, 1987.

Rexroth, Kenneth. *World Outside the Window: Selected Essays*. New York: New Directions, 1987.

Rich, Adrienne. "When We Dead Awaken: Writing as Re-Vision." In *Claims for Poetry*, edited by Donald Hall. Ann Arbor: University of Michigan Press, 1982.

Ricoeur, Paul. *History and Truth*. Evanston: University of Illinois Press, 1965.

Rilke, Rainer Maria. *Briefe aus Musot 1921–1926*. Leipzig: Insel-Verlag, 1935.

Rilke, Rainer Maria. *Briefe aus den Jahren 1914–1921*. Leipzig: Insel-

Verlag, 1937.

Rilke, Rainer Maria. *Rainer Maria Rilke—Lou Andreas Salome—Briefwechsel*. Zurich: Max Niehaus Verlag, 1952.

Rilke, Rainer Maria. *Sonnets to Orpheus*. Translated by Stephen Mitchell. New York: Simon and Schuster, 1985.

Rilke, Rainer Maria. *Selected Poetry*. Translated by Stephen Mitchell. New York: Random House, 1982.

Roethke, Theodore. *On the Poet and His Craft*. Edited by Ralph J. Mills, Jr. Seattle: University of Washington Press, 1966.

Rothenberg, Jerome. *Technicians of the Sacred: A Range of Poetries from Africa, America, Asia, Europe and Oceania*. Berkeley and Los Angeles: University of California Press, 1985.

Rumi, *Open Secret*. Translated by John Moyne and Coleman Barks. Putney, Vermont: Threshold Books, 1984.

Rumi, *Unseen Rain*. Translated by John Moyne and Coleman Barks. Putney, Vermont: Threshold Books, 1986.

Said, Edward W. *Orientalism*. New York: Vintage Books, 1979.

Said, Edward W. *The World, the Text, and the Critic*. Cambridge, Mass.: Harvard University Press, 1983.

Said, Edward W. "Opponents, Audiences, Constituencies, and Community." In *The Anti-Aesthetic*, edited by Hal Foster. Port Townsend, Washington: Bay Press, 1983.

Sarton, May. *I Knew a Phoenix: Sketches for an Autobiography*. New York: Rinehart, 1959.

Sartre, Jean-Paul. *The Words*. Translated by Bernard Frechtman. Greenwich, Conn: Fawcett, 1966.

Scott, F.R. *Collected Poems*. Toronto: McClelland & Stewart, 1981.

Scott, Peter Dale. "Anger and Poetic Politics in *Rock-Drill*." *San Jose Studies*, Fall 1986.

Scott, Peter Dale. "How Allen Dulles and the SS Preserved Each Other." *Covert Action*, Winter 1986.

Scott, Peter Dale. *Coming to Jakarta: A Poem About Terror*. New York: New Directions, 1989.

Scott, Peter Dale. "The Difference Perspective Makes." *Essays on Canadian Writing*, 1991.

Seagrave, Sterling. *The Marcos Dynasty*. New York: Harper and Row, 1988.

Seldes, Lee. *The Legacy of Mark Rothko*. New York: Holt, Rinehart and Winston, 1978.

Shaul, Sandra. *The Modern Image: Cubism and the Realist Tradition.* Edmonton: Edmonton Art Gallery, 1982.

Siegel, R.K., and Louis Jolyon West. *Hallucinations: Behavior, Experience, and Theory.* New York: Wiley, 1975.

Silliman, Ron. *New Sentence.* New York: Roof, 1987.

Simpson, Louis. *North of Jamaica.* New York: Harper and Row, 1972.

Singleton, Fred. *Twentieth-Century Yugoslavia.* London: Macmillan, 1976.

Smith, Bradley F., and Elena Agarossi. *Operation Sunrise.* New York: Basic Books, 1979.

Snyder, Gary. *Earth House Hold: Technical Notes & Queries To Fellow Dharma Revolutionaries.* New York: New Directions, 1968.

Snyder, Gary. *The Practice of the Wild.* San Francisco: North Point Press, 1990.

Steiner, George. *Language and Silence: Essays in Language, Literature and the Inhuman.* New York: Atheneum, 1977.

Stevens, Wallace. *The Necessary Angel: Essays on Reality and the Imagination.* London: Faber and Faber, 1960.

Stevenson, William. *Intrepid's Last Case.* New York: Villard Books, 1983.

Stirling, Brents. Introduction to "The Merchant of Venice." In *William Shakespeare: The Complete Works.* Edited by Alfred Harbage. Baltimore: Pelican, 1969.

Stockwell, John. *The Praetorian Guard: The U.S. Role in the New World Order.* Boston: South End Press, 1991.

Tolstoy, Leo. *War and Peace.* Translated by Contance Garnett. London: Dent, 1932.

Tomkins, Calvin. "A Reporter at Large: Irises." *The New Yorker,* April 4, 1988.

Truyen Kicu: *see* Du, Nguyen, *The Tale of Kieu.*

Tu Fu. *Selected Poems.* Translated by David Hinton. New York: New Directions, 1989.

Tworkov, Helen. *Zen in America: Profiles of Five Teachers.* San Francisco: North Point Press, 1989.

Van Gogh, Vincent. *Complete Letters.* Greenwich, Conn.: New York Graphic Society, n.d.

Vucinich, Wayne S., ed. *Contemporary Yugoslavia: Twenty Years of*

Socialist Experiment. Berkeley and Los Angeles: University of California Press, 1969.

Wang Wei. *The Poetry of Wang Wei: New Translations and Commentary*. Edited by Pauline Yu. Bloomington: Indiana University Press, 1980.

West, Louis Jolyon. *Hallucinations: A Symposium*. New York: Grune and Stratton, 1962.

Wilbur, Richard. *Responses. Prose Pieces: 1953–1976*. New York: Harcourt Brace Jovanovich, 1976.

Wilbur, Richard. "Poetry and Happiness" (1966). In *Claims for Poetry*, edited by Donald Hall. Ann Arbor: University of Michigan Press, 1982.

Woodcock, George. *Beyond the Blue Mountains: An Autobiography*. Markham, Ont: Fitzhenry and Whiteside, 1987.

Yeats, William Butler. *A Vision*. London: Macmillan, 1937.

Yeats, William Butler. *Variorum Edition of the Poems*. New York: Macmillan, 1957.

Yeats, William Butler. *Essays and Introductions*. London: Macmillan, 1961.

Yeats, William Butler. *Collected Poems*. New York: Macmillan, 1983.

Zinn, Howard. *A People's History of the United States*. New York: Harper and Row, 1980.

New Directions Paperbooks—A Partial Listing

Walter Abish, *How German Is It.* NDP508.
John Allman, *Scenarios for a Mixed Landscape.* NDP619.
Wayne Andrews, *The Surrealist Parade.* NDP689.
David Antin, *Tuning.* NDP570.
G. Apollinaire, *Selected Writings.*† NDP310.
Jimmy S. Baca, *Martín & Meditations.* NDP648.
  Black Mesa Poems. NDP676.
Djuna Barnes, *Nightwood.* NDP98.
J. Barzun, *An Essay on French Verse.* NDP708.
H.E. Bates, *Elephant's Nest in a Rhubarb Tree.* NDP669.
  A Party for the Girls, NDP653.
Charles Baudelaire, *Flowers of Evil.*† NDP684.
  Paris Spleen. NDP294.
Bei Dao, *Old Snow.* NDP727.
  Waves. NDP693.
Gottfried Benn, *Primal Vision.* NDP322.
Carmel Bird, *The Bluebird Café.* NDP707.
R. P. Blackmur, *Studies in Henry James,* NDP552.
Wolfgang Borchert, *The Man Outside.* NDP319.
Jorge Luis Borges, *Labyrinths.* NDP186.
  Seven Nights. NDP576.
Kay Boyle, *Life Being the Best.* NDP654.
  Three Short Novels. NDP703.
Buddha, *The Dhammapada.* NDP188.
M. Bulgakov, *Flight & Bliss.* NDP593.
  The Life of M. de Moliere. NDP601.
Frederick Busch, *Absent Friends.* NDP721.
Veza Canetti, *Yellow Street.* NDP709.
Ernesto Cardenal, *Zero Hour.* NDP502.
Joyce Cary, *A House of Children.* NDP631.
  Mister Johnson. NDP631.
Hayden Carruth, *Tell Me Again. . . .* NDP677.
Louis-Ferdinand Céline,
  Death on the Installment Plan. NDP330.
  Journey to the End of the Night. NDP542.
René Char. *Selected Poems.*† NDP734.
Jean Cocteau, *The Holy Terrors.* NDP212.
M. Collis, *She Was a Queen.* NDP716.
Cid Corman, *Sun Rock Man.* NDP318.
Gregory Corso, *Long Live Man.* NDP127.
  Herald of the Autochthonic Spirit. NDP522.
Robert Creeley, *Memory Gardens.* NDP613.
  Windows. NDP687.
Edward Dahlberg, *Because I Was Flesh.* NDP227.
Alain Daniélou, *The Way to the Labyrinth.* NDP634.
Osamu Dazai, *The Setting Sun.* NDP258.
  No Longer Human. NDP357.
Mme. de Lafayette, *The Princess of Cleves.* NDP660.
E. Dujardin, *We'll to the Woods No More.* NDP682.
Robert Duncan, *Ground Work.* NDP571.
  Ground Work II: In the Dark. NDP647.
Richard Eberhart, *The Long Reach.* NDP565.
Wm. Empson, *7 Types of Ambiguity.* NDP204.
  Some Versions of Pastoral. NDP92.
S. Endo, *Stained Glass Elegies.* NDP699.
Wm. Everson, *The Residual Years.* NDP263.
Gavin Ewart, *Selected Poems.* NDP655
Lawrence Ferlinghetti, *Endless Life.* NDP516.
  A Coney Island of the Mind. NDP74.
  European Poems & Transitions. NDP582
  Starting from San Francisco. NDP220.
  Wild Dreams of a New Beginning. NDP663.
Ronald Firbank, *Five Novels.* NDP581.
  Three More Novels. NDP614.
F. Scott Fitzgerald, *The Crack-up.* NDP54.
Gustave Flaubert, *Dictionary.* NDP230.
J. Gahagan, *Did Gustav Mahler Ski?* NDP711.
Gandhi, *Gandhi on Non-Violence.* NDP197.
Gary, Romain, *Promise at Dawn.* NDP635.
  The Life Before Us ("Madame Rosa"). NDP604.
W. Gerhardie, *Futility.* NDP722.
Goethe, *Faust,* Part I. NDP70.
Henry Green, *Back.* NDP517
Allen Grossman, *The Ether Dome.* NDP723.
Martin Grzimek, *Shadowlife.* NDP705.
Guigonnat, Henri, *Daemon in Lithuania.* NDP592.
Lars Gustafsson, *The Death of a Beekeeper.* NDP523.
  Stories of Happy People. NDP616.

John Hawkes, *The Beetle Leg.* NDP239.
  Humors of Blood & Skin. NDP577.
  Second Skin. NDP146.
Samuel Hazo, *To Paris.* NDP512.
H. D. *Collected Poems.* NDP611.
  The Gift. NDP546.
  Helen in Egypt. NDP380.
  HERmione. NDP526.
  Selected Poems. NDP658.
  Tribute to Freud. NDP572.
Robert E. Helbling, *Heinrich von Kleist.* NDP390.
William Herrick, *Love and Terror.* NDP538.
Herman Hesse, *Siddhartha.* NDP65.
Paul Hoover, *The Novel.* NDP706.
Vicente Huidobro, *Selected Poetry.* NDP520.
C. Isherwood, *All the Conspirators.* NDP480.
  The Berlin Stories. NDP134.
Ledo Ivo, *Snake's Nest.* NDP521.
Gustav Janouch, *Conversations with Kafka.* NDP313.
Alfred Jarry, *Ubu Roi.* NDP105.
Robinson Jeffers, *Cawdor and Medea.* NDP293.
B.S. Johnson, *Christie Malry's. . . .* NDP600.
  Albert Angelo. NDP628.
James Joyce, *Stephen Hero.* NDP133.
Franz Kafka, *Amerika.* NDP117.
Bob Kaufman, *The Ancient Rain.* NDP514.
H. von Kleist, *Prince Friedrich.* NDP462.
Shimpei Kusano, *Asking Myself. . . .* NDP566.
Jules Laforgue, *Moral Tales.* NDP594.
P. Lal, *Great Sanskrit Plays.* NDP142.
Tommaso Landolfi, *Gogol's Wife.* NDP155.
  "Language" Poetries: An Anthology. NDP630.
D. Larsen, *Stitching Porcelain.* NDP710.
Lautréamont, *Maldoror.* NDP207.
Irving Layton, *Selected Poems.* NDP431.
Christine Lehner, *Expecting.* NDP544.
H. Leibowitz, *Fabricating Lives.* NDP715.
Siegfried Lenz, *The German Lesson.* NDP618.
Denise Levertov, *Breathing the Water.* NDP640.
  Candles in Babylon. NDP533.
  A Door in the Hive. NDP685.
  Poems 1960-1967. NDP549.
  Poems 1968-1972. NDP629.
  Oblique Prayers. NDP578.
Harry Levin, *James Joyce.* NDP87.
Li Ch'ing-chao, *Complete Poems.* NDP492.
Enrique Lihn, *The Dark Room.*† NDP542.
C. Lispector, *Soulstorm.* NDP671.
  The Hour of the Star. NDP733.
García Lorca, *Five Plays.* NDP232
  The Public & Play Without a Title. NDP561.
  Selected Poems.† NDP114
  Three Tragedies. NDP52.
Francisco G. Lorca, *In The Green Morning.* NDP610.
Michael McClure, *Rebel Lions.* NDP712.
  Selected Poems. NDP599.
Carson McCullers, *The Member of the Wedding.* (Playscript) NDP153.
Stéphane Mallarmé,† *Selected Poetry and Prose.* NDP529.
Thomas Merton, *Asian Journal.* NDP394.
  New Seeds of Contemplation. ND337.
  Selected Poems. NDP85.
  Thomas Merton in Alaska. NDP652.
  The Way of Chuang Tzu. NDP276.
  The Wisdom of the Desert. NDP295.
  Zen and the Birds of Appetite. NDP261.
Henri Michaux, *A Barbarian in Asia.* NDP622.
  Selected Writings. NDP264.
Henry Miller, *The Air-Conditioned Nightmare.* NDP302.
  Big Sur & The Oranges. NDP161.
  The Colossus of Maroussi. NDP75.
  Into the Heart of Life. NDP728.
  The Smile at the Foot of the Ladder. NDP386.
  Stand Still Like the Hummingbird. NDP236.
  The Time of the Assassins. NDP115.
Y. Mishima, *Confessions of a Mask.* NDP253.
  Death in Midsummer. NDP215.

For complete listing request free catalog from
New Directions, 80 Eighth Avenue, New York 10011

†Bilingual

Frédéric Mistral, *The Memoirs.* NDP632.
Eugenio Montale, *It Depends.*† NDP507.
  Selected Poems.† NDP193.
Paul Morand, *Fancy Goods / Open All Night.*
  NDP567.
Vladimir Nabokov, *Nikolai Gogol.* NDP78.
  Laughter in the Dark. NDP729.
  The Real Life of Sebastian Knight. NDP432.
P. Neruda, *The Captain's Verses.*† NDP345.
  Residence on Earth.† NDP340.
New Directions in Prose & Poetry (Anthology).
  Available from #17 forward to #55.
Robert Nichols, *Arrival.* NDP437.
  Exile. NDP485.
J. F. Nims, *The Six-Cornered Snowflake.* NDP700.
Charles Olson, *Selected Writings.* NDP231.
Toby Olson, *The Life of Jesus.* NDP417.
  Seaview. NDP532.
George Oppen, *Collected Poems.* NDP418.
István Örkeny, *The Flower Show /*
  The Toth Family. NDP536.
Wilfred Owen, *Collected Poems.* NDP210.
José Emilio Pacheco, *Battles in the Desert.* NDP637.
  Selected Poems.† NDP638.
Nicanor Parra, *Antipoems: New & Selected.* NDP603.
Boris Pasternak, *Safe Conduct.* NDP77.
Kenneth Patchen, *Aflame and Afun.* NDP292.
  Because It Is. NDP83.
  Collected Poems. NDP284.
  Hallelujah Anyway. NDP219.
  Selected Poems. NDP160.
Ota Pavel, *How I Came to Know Fish.* NDP713.
Octavio Paz, *Collected Poems.* NDP719.
  Configurations.† NDP303.
  A Draft of Shadows.† NDP489.
  Selected Poems. NDP574.
  Sunstone.† NDP735.
  A Tree Within.† NDP661.
St. John Perse, *Selected Poems.*† NDP545.
J. A. Porter, *Eelgrass.* NDP438.
Ezra Pound, *ABC of Reading.* NDP89.
  Confucius. NDP285.
  Confucius to Cummings. (Anth.) NDP126.
  A Draft of XXX Cantos. NDP690.
  Elektra. NDP683.
  Guide to Kulchur. NDP257.
  Literary Essays. NDP250.
  Personae. NDP697.
  Selected Cantos. NDP304.
  Selected Poems. NDP66.
  The Spirit of Romance. NDP266.
  Translations.† (Enlarged Edition) NDP145.
Raymond Queneau, *The Blue Flowers.* NDP595.
  Exercises in Style. NDP513.
Mary de Rachewiltz, *Ezra Pound.* NDP405.
Raja Rao, *Kanthapura.* NDP224.
Herbert Read, *The Green Child.* NDP208.
P. Reverdy, *Selected Poems.*† NDP346.
Kenneth Rexroth, *An Autobiographical Novel.* NDP725.
  Classics Revisited. NDP621.
  More Classics Revisited. NDP668.
  Flower Wreath Hill. NDP724.
  100 Poems from the Chinese. NDP192.
  100 Poems from the Japanese.† NDP147.
  Selected Poems. NDP581.
  Women Poets of China. NDP528.
  Women Poets of Japan. NDP527.
Rainer Maria Rilke, *Poems from*
  The Book of Hours. NDP408.
  Possibility of Being. (Poems). NDP436.
  Where Silence Reigns. (Prose). NDP464.
Arthur Rimbaud, *Illuminations.*† NDP56.
  Season in Hell & Drunken Boat.† NDP97.
Edouard Roditi, *Delights of Turkey.* NDP445.
Jerome Rothenberg, *Khurbn.* NDP679.
  New Selected Poems. NDP625.
Nayantara Sahgal, *Rich Like Us.* NDP665.
Saigyo, *Mirror for the Moon.*† NDP465.

Ihara Saikaku, *The Life of an Amorous*
  Woman. NDP270.
St. John of the Cross, *Poems.*† NDP341.
W. Saroyan, *Madness in the Family.* NDP691.
Jean-Paul Sartre, *Nausea.* NDP82.
  The Wall (Intimacy). NDP272.
P. D. Scott, *Coming to Jakarta.* NDP672.
Delmore Schwartz, *Selected Poems.* NDP241.
  Last & Lost Poems. NDP673.
  In Dreams Begin Responsibilities. NDP454.
Shattan, *Manimekhalaï.* NDP674.
K. Shiraishi. *Seasons of Sacred Lust.* NDP453.
Stevie Smith, *Collected Poems.* NDP562.
  New Selected Poems. NDP659.
Gary Snyder, *The Back Country.* NDP249.
  The Real Work. NDP499.
  Regarding Wave. NDP306.
  Turtle Island. NDP381.
Enid Starkie, *Rimbaud.* NDP254.
Stendhal. *Three Italian Chronicles.* NDP704.
Antonio Tabucchi, *Indian Nocturne.* NDP666.
Nathaniel Tarn, *Lyrics . . . Bride of God.* NDP391.
Dylan Thomas, *Adventures in the Skin Trade.*
  NDP183.
  A Child's Christmas in Wales. NDP181.
  Collected Poems 1934-1952. NDP316.
  Collected Stories. NDP626.
  Portrait of the Artist as a Young Dog. NDP51.
  Quite Early One Morning. NDP90.
  Under Milk Wood. NDP73.
Tian Wen: *A Chinese Book of Origins.* NDP624.
Uwe Timm, *The Snake Tree.* NDP686.
Lionel Trilling, *E. M. Forster.* NDP189.
Tu Fu, *Selected Poems.* NDP675.
N. Tucci, *The Rain Came Last.* NDP688.
Martin Turnell, *Baudelaire.* NDP336.
Paul Valéry, *Selected Writings.*† NDP184.
Elio Vittorini, *A Vittorini Omnibus.* NDP366.
Rosmarie Waldrop, *The Reproduction of Profiles.*
  NDP649.
Robert Penn Warren, *At Heaven's Gate.* NDP588.
Vernon Watkins, *Selected Poems.* NDP221.
Eliot Weinberger, *Works on Paper.* NDP627.
Nathanael West, *Miss Lonelyhearts &*
  Day of the Locust. NDP125.
J. Wheelwright, *Collected Poems.* NDP544.
Tennessee Williams, *Baby Doll.* NDP714.
  Camino Real. NDP301.
  Cat on a Hot Tin Roof. NDP398.
  Clothes for a Summer Hotel. NDP556.
  The Glass Menagerie. NDP218.
  Hard Candy. NDP225.
  In the Winter of Cities. NDP154.
  A Lovely Sunday for Creve Coeur. NDP497.
  One Arm & Other Stories. NDP237.
  Red Devil Battery Sign. NDP650.
  A Streetcar Named Desire. NDP501.
  Sweet Bird of Youth. NDP409.
  Twenty-Seven Wagons Full of Cotton. NDP217.
  Vieux Carre. NDP482.
William Carlos Williams,
  The Autobiography. NDP223.
  The Buildup. NDP259.
  Collected Poems: Vol. I. NDP730.
  Collected Poems: Vol. II. NDP731.
  The Doctor Stories. NDP585.
  Imaginations. NDP329.
  In the American Grain. NDP53.
  In the Money. NDP240.
  Paterson. Complete. NDP152.
  Pictures from Brueghel. NDP118.
  Selected Poems (new ed.). NDP602.
  White Mule. NDP226.
Wisdom Books: *Early Buddhists.* NDP444;
  Spanish Mystics. NDP442; *St. Francis.* NDP477;
  Taoists. NDP509; *Wisdom of the Desert.* NDP295;
  Zen Masters. NDP415.

For complete listing request free catalog from
New Directions, 80 Eighth Avenue, New York 10011   †Bilingual